Food Crops from your Garden or Allotment

Brian Furner is a Fellow of the Linnean Society of London and a member of the Soil Association. In the gardening world he is well known as a vegetable specialist – all the vegetables and most of the fruit he eats are grown in his garden and on his allotment in Kent – and in particular as an exponent of up-to-date, labour-saving methods. He has studied horticulture as far afield as Israel and Morocco and keeps in touch with research stations in the USA and Russia. He is the author of several gardening books, including *The Kitchen Garden*, also published by Pan Books, and has contributed to various gardening magazines for many years.

Also available in the Small Garden Series

Small Garden Series
Editor C. E. Lucas Phillips

Brian Furner
Food Crops from your Garden or Allotment

plates from photographs taken by the author

Pan Original Pan Books London and Sydney

First published 1976 by Pan Books Ltd,
Cavaye Place, London SW10 9PG
© Brian Furner 1976
ISBN 0 330 24785 9
Printed in Great Britain by
Richard Clay (The Chaucer Press) Ltd
Bungay, Suffolk

Contents

1 Home or away?

This book has just one aim: to help you to grow healthy fruit and vegetables. It is so important, I think, that home-grown fruit and vegetables should be produced as cheaply as possible. I have done my best to explain how this can be done. Where possible, I have also suggested how routine garden work can be reduced. But to grow fruit and vegetables which not only taste good but look good calls for quite a bit of work on your part. Far better, I believe, to grow a few home food crops well than to try to grow a lot and have mediocre results. I grew all the fruit and vegetables I eat for more than twenty years without having any real garden at all. I had (and still have) an allotment. If you already have an allotment or are thinking of applying for one I hope that you will find some of my suggestions of use and I am assuming that you may well be a beginner to home food crop growing. Please bear that point in mind if you already grow fruit and vegetables and wonder why I sometimes go into some detail to explain something which to you is already commonplace. If you already practise methods which lead to excellent crops, carry on by these methods. On the other hand, by all means try out any of my methods if you feel they may save you time, work and money.

The absolute beginner may feel that, for the production of good fruit and vegetables, there is little to do but to dig over a part of the garden and to plant or sow. This can be done and crops can be excellent. More often things go wrong; sometimes very wrong. None of the fruits and vegetables we grow in our gardens likes having its roots surrounded for a long time by water. Badly-drained soil is quite useless for the growing of fruit and vegetables and improving drainage is difficult unless you know something about land drains and gradients. If you take on the job of laying drains, remember that the surplus water has to run somewhere . . .

not into a neighbour's garden, for instance! It would be wiser in most cases to call in a contractor specializing in the necessary work. In London, the classified Yellow Pages telephone directory has a section on garden contractors. Your own local telephone directory may have a similar section; a local garden centre may be able to give you names and addresses of local contractors.

A good many people have soils which are very *heavy*. In gardener's jargon this means a soil with a high proportion of clay. Digging heavy soils can be hard work as they retain water well. This means that in summer, garden crops in heavy soils need far less attention as regards watering than do those in *light* soils which contain quite a lot of sand or gravel. But heavy soils often drain badly, so badly in fact that for many months of the year far too much water remains around the roots of garden-grown fruits and vegetables. The gardener is usually advised to open up a heavy soil by digging large quantities of bulky farmyard manure into it. Similar advice is proffered to the gardener with a light soil as farmyard manure gives a light soil 'body' so that the soil does not dry out rapidly in dry summer spells. The advice is sound until one considers the cost of the vast quantities of manure. In all my years of gardening I have had to deal with very light soils. Instead of farmyard manure, I have made and used vast quantities of garden compost, costing me nothing apart from my own time and energy. Cut your costs by using garden compost instead of expensive (and not always of first-class quality) farmyard manure.

Some gardening experts would still have us all digging our gardens deeply. Excellent advice, too, for keeping down the waist line but not always for getting excellent crops. In the old days deep digging provided work for the second gardener and the under-gardener in winter. The soils of kitchen gardens of stately homes had been well-manured and worked for generations. Regular deep digging of the soils did no harm; whether it did any good is another matter. But how many of our gardens have soils like that? If I dig down a foot, I strike gravel. Even unluckier are many gardeners on new housing estates. If they dig down a foot or so they may strike builders' rubble or any of the materials dumped years before to fill a sandpit or level off an area of waste land. Some deep digging is called for if you have to dig through and break a band of clay running a foot or so below the soil surface. If you have to carry out any deep digging to improve soil drainage, try to prevent the lower, less fertile soil from ending up on top.

When farmyard manure was used in huge quantities to improve and retain the physical condition of soils and to make them very fertile, it was necessary to neutralize excess acidity in the manure by spreading lime fairly often and generously. Garden compost is more or less neutral and where soils are fed with this home-made manure the liming of the garden soil is usually not necessary. Garden compost is excellent food for earthworms – very important soil inhabitants that manufacture and excrete lime.

Our garden fruits and vegetables abhor very acidic soil conditions and if your garden soil is acidic you may have to apply lime at the outset. Reasonably priced soil testing gadgets are on sale at garden shops and in chain stores to check your soil for acidity. If lime is needed to neutralize excess soil acidity, a safe dose of carbonate of lime (ground chalk) is 250 gramme to the sq m ($\frac{1}{2}$ lb to the sq yd). Lime may also be sprinkled on to layers of wastes as you add them to the compost heap and should suffice to reduce soil acidity.

How to deal with a large and weedy garden or allotment when a start is being made poses some problems. Chemical weedkillers have no place in the kitchen garden or on an allotment site. Hiring a flame gun may seem a good idea but is just as bad as building a bonfire with all of the top growth of grasses and weeds. The top growth has in it many of the plant foods and trace elements (minerals needed for the good growth and health of plants but in extremely small quantities) taken from the soil by the roots. There are several ways of tackling this initial job. But, first of all, what sort of weed growth is it? A garden or allotment which has been neglected for about a year may be covered with a dense growth of annual weeds like shepherd's purse, small nettle, groundsel and chickweed. All of these are shallow rooting. Among them there may be the occasional dandelion and dock. Tackling weedy soil in this state is easy. Just dig it, removing all weeds and weed roots as you do so. Put the weeds on the compost heap. If the few docks and dandelions are not killed by the heat engendered by fermentation, spot them when digging in or spreading the compost and add the weeds to the next compost heap. A garden fork is usually the best tool to use when clearing the soil of weeds.

Then we come to the large garden or allotment which has become so neglected that it resembles waste land. Apart from the many docks and dandelions and a patch of stinging nettle – easy-to-get-rid-of perennial weeds – there may be garden horrors like ground elder, common horse-tail and bindweed and a thick mat of couch grass. I have had to clear land of this sort on several occasions. My own way of doing the job is to strip off 'turves' 2·5 cm (1 in) or so thick and to pile them in large stacks. The stacks rot down to leave what resembles potting soil within two to three years. Decomposition is hastened if you cover each stack with a large sheet of black polythene. I then dig the entire area to a depth of about 12–15 cm (5–6 ins), using a garden fork. If it is summer and the weather warm, I leave the dug out roots of the weed growth removed during the digging to dry out before adding them to a stack of turfy weeds. In winter I burn the roots. After decomposition the entire stack (apart from any weed growth on its exterior) should be spread back on top of the ground. However infertile the soil itself may be after the initial digging, I ensure that my first crops will have sufficient food for good growth by using garden compost at the rate of a large barrowload per square metre (or square yard). After planting potatoes, I spread compost as a mulch (soil cover). With winter greens the compost mulch is spread before planting. And so on. In the first season I pull up or dig out (using a hand fork) every piece of weed root which shoots. The entire site is dug and any weed growth removed before the next season's crops are sown or planted, and more garden compost is applied for potatoes and winter greens. Residues in the dug in compost (dug in to a depth of only a few centimetres) provide sufficient plant foods for carrots, beetroot, lettuce, radish, spring onions, maincrop onions from sets, shallots, summer cabbage and several other vegetables.

Annual weeds are not a great problem if you keep pace with them and never let them smother vegetable seedlings, otherwise clearing them becomes an almost impossible task. Planting fruits (apart from strawberries) should not be undertaken until ground is free from garden horrors.

But this initial weed clearance is really not feasible in a small garden in which there is no room for even a small stack of turfy weeds. If you are faced with the job of cleaning a small patch of wasteland I suggest you simply dig the entire garden to a depth of 12–15 cm (5–6 ins), tugging at the roots of perennials as you do so. In summer, dig deeply around dandelions and docks in order to remove the roots, otherwise they will break off or you may dislocate your arm! Although the burning of the weeds leads to a loss of valuable plant foods, bonfiring may be the easiest and best answer when dealing with a small garden badly infested with perennial weeds. For a bed of stinging nettles, cut down the top growth if it is summer and add it to the compost heap. There is no better native wild plant for compost-making than the stinging nettle. Stinging nettles grow only in soil which is highly fertile; soil without them will need a lot of compost. After digging out the roots and burning them you may sow and plant vegetables, knowing that crops should be good. Have garden compost ready to hand or build a compost heap now so that you can feed the hungry soil and make a start at growing food crops.

Perhaps you have no garden of your own or only a very small one, yet you wish to grow more fruit and vegetables. Perhaps the garden next door or just up the road just isn't cultivated and you are thinking of asking to use it. The idea is a good one but there are perils. After you have done the hard work, will the owner wish to take over from you? Have the owners left the garden to its sad fate because they are considering moving house? Is the old lady with the weedy garden ill? When she dies will you be able to continue your good work in her garden? These points and others are worth considering before you suggest or accept an offer to take over a neighbour's garden.

Taking on an allotment may involve rather similar considerations. Never, unless you are willing to take the plunge, take on what is known as a 'temporary allotment'. Temporary allotments are sited on land scheduled for development at an unknown date. Seeing a vacant plot of land nearby and knowing that the local authority is very willing to have the site tidied up by you and cultivated by you as an allotment does seem a tempting invitation to get cracking and produce tasty, home-grown foods.

But after you have cleared the site, fertilized the soil and started to get good crops, along may come a Notice to Quit. My first temporary allotment was buried under 20 feet of household rubbish; my second coated with a 2-foot layer of concrete.

Temporary allotments are bound to be offered by private land-owners just as soon as more and more people decide that growing food has the advantages which you and I know it has. I suggest you discuss any contract with a solicitor before signing it. Local authorities issue contracts to tenants of plots on the authorities' permanent allotment sites. To get a plot these days almost in-variably means putting your name on the waiting list. But do not be fobbed off by a local official's letter or statement that all of the plots on your local site are tenanted. Go to the site and check for yourself. You may well come across several plots which have obviously not been cultivated for years. Go back to the council offices armed with this knowledge. Explain to officials there the position of the uncultivated plots. A helpful local authority will have an official willing to visit the site and check what you have discovered. A local authority's records about allotments can be in a shocking muddle. Before taking on an allotment at all have a family discussion. Most plots average 301 sq m (300 sq yds) or in allotment language 10 rods. This area may not sound large: start digging and cultivating and you will find that it is. Will your family share the work with you? Do you know of any sources of waste products like piles of weeds or grass cuttings and will any-one help to collect them for your first large compost heap? If the total area is a bit too much to cultivate well have you a neighbour who will share the work or cultivate half of your plot and, of course, receive half the resultant crops? How far is the plot from your home? If it is five minutes away by car that seems fine. But how far is it away if you decide to sell the car? Have you the time or will you make the time to spend the major part of each weekend between say late March and August on your plot? Will you be free in the evenings in spring and early summer when allotment work with vegetables has to be regular? Are you fit enough to carry out annual digging and possibly to haul 250 kgs ($\frac{1}{4}$ ton) of water in cans around the plot on a dry summer day? Is the allotment site noted as a thieves' paradise? Have a chat with one or two plot-holders there. It is a waste of time taking an allotment if a lot of the produce will be stolen. What other hazards are there? Let me explain what I mean.

When I moved to my present allotment, sited on a local permanent site, I found it littered with bottles, cans – even a kitchen sink. That sort of thing is no problem. Any local authority can be pushed to collect such refuse if the plot-holder insists firmly and piles the stuff in a tidy heap. The site was not fenced but thieving of produce was almost negligible. But stray dogs wandered at will over the waste land which was to be my allotment. To stop that sort of worry I erected a 1·2-m (4-ft) high fence round the site; the local authority did not object so I raised the fence by another 60 cm (2 ft) to make an excellent trellis for runner beans (see page 38) or blackberries (see page 138). There was no water supply and I had a difficult problem keeping vegetables from dying through a lack of soil moisture in the first summer. Then the local authority took it into its head to link the plot site with piped water which has to be collected from steel tanks – time-consuming, hard work if your plot is at some distance from a tank. The local authority also decided to fence the site and to issue keys to tenants. Wood pigeons were a menace to winter greenstuff. Instead of letting them devour my greens I stretched protective netting above the winter cabbages, sprouts and broccoli. One of the plot-holders told me that slugs ruined many vegetables in a wet summer. I saw what these pests could do when I dug my potato crop in the second season. But frogs and toads devour slugs. Local boys gave me a couple of dozen large frogs and a lot of frog spawn. The frogs were released on the plot and a small, shallow pond dug and lined with a pool liner for the tadpoles which we fed on goldfish food, brown bread and lamb chop bones. Other plot-holders were asked to stop using persistent pesticides which could harm the frogs and new tenants were asked not to burn any weedy top growth in which the growing frog population spent the winter. We still have slugs but not in plague proportions.

Getting to my plot was another problem. There was no path from the site entrance to any plot. I dug and carted off the hillocks of soil and weeds which barred my way to my plot, levelled off and laid metre-wide black plastic sheeting over the new path. After I had finished, several other plot holders as well as I could walk along or wheel barrows from the site entrance to our plots. I explain all of this because one must be prepared to take a hand and not expect the local authority to carry out every improvement on a site. The annual rental for a 10-rod plot with water may be as low as £2 or as high as the local authority decides. The terms form part of the agreement between tenant and local authority. Study the terms well before you sign although there is little you can do to get a local authority to change them. Note how many months' notice you have to give the council if you wish to vacate the plot and note, too, if the council includes clauses which (at first sight) appear pettyfogging – no children allowed on the site is an example. Many plot-holders wisely (I think) ignore clauses of this sort. Children can find an allotment a boring place. This can be rectified if the weekend trip to the allotment is coupled with all the trappings of a countryside picnic. The agreement may lay down specifications regarding the size of the shed you want to erect on your allotment. There may be no regulations at all regarding the erection of a greenhouse. It would be worth checking with the council if you wish to have one on your allotment. Any regulation which says you must not grow flowers is rather out of date these days.

Most gardeners like to take over an allotment in winter so that the initial clearance can be carried out before spring sowings and plantings are due. But an allotment may be started at any time, provided that the gardener knows that a plot taken over in summer or autumn cannot be expected to produce much in the way of food crops that same season. I have so often heard new plot-holders complain bitterly that the local authority should have churned up the weedy plot initially. That the authority has not is in reality a blessing. New plot-holders seldom know that mechanical gardening machinery cannot distinguish between annual and perennial weeds. So the whole area can be churned up and the roots of perennials chopped into many small sections, each of which (notably on couch grass, bindweed, goutweed, common horse-tail) quickly becomes a new young plant, leading to a great deal of extra work.

The taking of waste land (or garden lawn for that matter) into cultivation upsets the balance of nature. Below the soil surface are the many small forms of life which fit in with nature's plan. You will meet earthworms as you remove weed growth and dig; a healthy, fertile soil contains many monster-sized worms. Treat them with respect as they improve soil drainage and do other helpful jobs. Here and there a quick-moving centipede or devil's coach horse evades your spade or fork. Never harm these creatures. You will learn to recognize the slow-moving millepede (not really a pest, although so often said to be one) and the very sluggish wireworm 1–2·5-cm ($\frac{1}{2}$–1-in) long, reddish brown or yellowish brown and hard to the touch, the equally sluggish caterpillar-like off-white or brownish cutworms and leather-jackets. Digging and hoeing expose these pests to garden allot-ment birds. Remove and kill any of this latter group as you cultivate. Baiting wireworms with pieces of carrot or potato can help. Skewer the vegetable pieces and bury them a few centimetres below ground. Dig up the skewered pieces every few days and re-move and kill the wireworms eating the carrot. Remember, you have removed the natural sources of food of these soil inhabiters. Without the tasty roots and top growth of weeds these 'pests' turn to your vegetable plants as a source of food.

The mini-garden

Although this book deals with the production of fruits and vege-tables in gardens as well as on allotments, I have pointed out here and there that a subject is worth growing if your garden is no more than a paved back-yard, a town balcony or a window-box necessitating the use of containers. Having to buy suitable pots may seem expensive. It can be, but bear in mind that you need use the pots or tubs for food crops for no more than six months of the year. For the rest of the year – late autumn, winter and spring – the containers may house spring bulbs. So you get two different and valuable uses from them. Of course, you can do things even more cheaply if you grow vegetables and herbs in disused plastic buckets. Always remember to make a few drainage holes in the bottom of them. An easy way of making drainage holes in brittle plastic is to heat a poker until it is red hot and to push it through the bottom of the bucket here and there.

Good gardening and enjoy it!

2 Planning for plenty

The quantity of fresh produce you will harvest depends on, among other things, the total area of land cultivated for fruit and vegetables. As I have said, it is far better to cultivate a small garden or even one allotment really well than to try to cope with too much. I hope I have stressed that the production of food crops does not consist, more or less, of digging up any old piece of ground, sowing and planting and leaving things to come along as best they can. Careful attention to details of cultivation is very necessary. This does not mean a slavish regard to the system of cultivation in this book or in any other work on the subject. Devise your own ways of doing things and, above all, try to cut down on all unnecessary work. But whether the total area is large or small, the soil itself must be of high fertility. Your chances of taking over a garden or allotment with a soil of high fertility rating are small. Start thinking about soil-rejuvenation and how the soil fertility rating can be increased. If you are starting off with a small kitchen garden in what is already a reasonably well cultivated garden devoted to shrubs and flowering plants, you can plan ahead as regards improving the soil fertility of the plot where food crops are to be grown even before making a start on digging and clearing the area. When you decide to go in for fruit and vegetable growing, start compost-making like mad! Apart from weeds and remains of plants like dahlia foliage in autumn, make sure that all household wastes are conserved for compost-making. I have a bin just outside the kitchen door, into which goes anything and everything which has once had life. If you are scared of attracting rats, foxes or stray cats and dogs you will wisely not include remnants of cooked food in your compost heaps. But if your dog consumes most of the kitchen scraps there will be little surplus anyway, and this may be buried within the garden soil and at a depth (say 30 cm or 1 ft) where scavengers will not get at it. The daily newspaper (after the family has done with it), tea leaves, potato peelings, trimmings from cabbage and lettuce, pea pods, vacuum-cleaner dust . . . in fact anything of an organic nature is useful material for the compost heap. Years ago discarded clothing was suitable for compost-making; now most clothing is entirely or in part manufactured with man-made fibres and not of use in compost-making. I empty my compost bin on to the heap at least once each week in cooler weather; more frequently in summer. If you have a bin of this sort, ensure that refuse collectors respect it. You do not wish them to walk off with your precious wastes when they take away really unwanted household wastes like tin cans, plastic containers and ash from coal or smokeless fuel fires. For the gardener who has no real garden but who has an allotment, all household organic wastes need transferring to the plot. Polythene sacks come in handy for the stuff to be taken to the allotment.

One's own weeds and wastes are insufficient to build large, very desirable compost heaps, but it is amazing just how many varied wastes there are around and for free. The country gardener frequently has the opportunity of getting cut grass and weeds left on roadside verges, spoilt hay from a farmer's field and unwanted grass mowings and weeds from neighbouring gardens. The suburban gardener may also discover suitable wastes in plenty. The large lawn and small flower border sort of neighbour is delighted to hand over or have lawn mowings and garden weeds collected regularly. Regularity is important. For many gardeners a heap of mowings and weeds is a nasty, smelly, unwanted object to be burned (where possible) or to be added in small quantities to the refuse bin. When I took over my present allotment I quite quickly saw a potential rich source of garden wastes for my compost heaps and supplied each household near the allotment site with one or more strong plastic sacks in which to place all organic wastes and hand them over to me. Of course, on my part, I am happy to hand over some of the allotment-grown fruit and veg. This sort of arrangement works well. Town gardeners may feel they really have little hope of supplies of extra wastes for compost-making. But there are always local lawn enthusiasts eager to dispose of mowings and a town greengrocer happy to have his own smelly wastes taken away regularly. I have never had a working arrangement with local shops but there must be many with wastes worth considering. Smelly wastes of the fish/butcher sort would be ideal in *large* compost heaps on commercial holdings. Factory waste products are also of greater use to the farmer and commercial man. Any heap of organic waste will rot down to compost in due course and the resultant product is not to be despised.

But the home food grower aims at having compost as soon as possible and having a home-made, cost-free manure containing all plant foods and most of the trace elements which our garden plants must have if their growth is to be optimum. Britain is a great importer of food and other organic matter. Vast quantities of wastes from these imports contain plant foods and trace elements – something which has not yet struck the nation's food growers and the nation's government. But many gardeners are fully aware that these wastes are very valuable. Garden compost is enhanced by the inclusion in the compost heap of as many varied wastes as we can possibly lay our hands on. 'Scrounging' is not the right word to use when on the look out for suitable organic wastes for the compost heap. You must feel you are doing a service, not only in improving the physical quality of your garden or allotment soil but in also carrying out useful conservation work. Burying in order to fill in sand, gravel and chalk pits is ethical although this use of valuable waste products puts them deeply out of the way of the roots of most farm and garden crops; burning and sea disposal is sheer pollution of our planet.

Small quantities of animal dung are added to compost heaps. The dung supplies some nitrogenous salts which are of use to the billions of bacteria and fungi which break down wastes. The country gardener should be able to get small quantities of animal dung relatively easily and at no charge. Cow and horse manure are slowly becoming saleable commodities and can be obtained from a friendly local farmer. The suburban and town gardener may feel that getting small quantities of dung is difficult. This need not be so. Neighbours with pet rabbits, guinea pigs and hens may be disposing of a great deal of droppings via the council's refuse collection service. Then there are the pigeon fanciers. They just do not know what to do with the relatively vast quantities of droppings in pigeon lofts. If you wish to link up with local pigeon racers, note their names and addresses on baskets returned to your railway station or ask railway staff for these details. But here again I must stress the importance of regularity of collection. A pigeon fancier has no wish to be saddled with several sacks of dung, eggs and dead bodies awaiting collection at your leisure.

It amazes me that so few gardeners make compost well and quickly. Some gardeners never seem to cotton on to how a compost heap should be made and many a heap of wastes is so dry that it is eventually set alight. Other heaps turn out to be unpleasant, smelly and greasy after having stood for a year or more. To make good compost rapidly and well involves some understanding of the process by which bacteria and fungi break down organic wastes. Warmth is necessary. Compost heaps made on the grand scale on commercial holdings are likely to retain engendered heat well, and such large heaps may not need protection.

It is not possible to make monster heaps in our gardens or on our allotments but we can assist a medium-sized heap to retain heat by either constructing the pile in a bin or covering the heap on its completion. Here again, do not be misled into thinking that you have to copy what I say here or what others do. By all means base your method on my methods, and then adapt them. Here in the garden I have a compost bin made of wood. It is a Huker bin measuring 100 × 100 cm (40 × 40 ins) and 80 cm (32 ins) high (see diagram). The wood was treated with a copper fungicide by the makers and I would expect it to have a life of at least ten years. The gaps between the slats admit air – a requisite in the early stages of decomposition of the wastes. An advantage of this sort of bin is its mobility. I can use it all winter and stack it away behind the shed in summer when I have a permanent bin at the far end of the garden consisting of two sheets of corrugated asbestos each measuring 1·8 × 0·7 m (6 × 2 ft). These sheets set at 1·2 m (4 ft) apart are supported by scrap iron poles hammered into the ground. A third sheet of asbestos serves as the back of the 'box'. At the front there is another asbestos sheet which may be taken away when a heap is being made, replaced when the heap is completed and taken away again when the compost is being dug out. I take care that wastes placed in this bin are not too wet. Lack of air could lead to putrefaction rather than fermentation. On the allotments I use the American Black Sheet way of compost-making. This is not an attractive way of making garden compost but allotment sites are not noted for beauty. The blessing of the Black Sheet method is that, like the Huker box

method, a compost heap can be made anywhere on the site. This is handy. After all, if you want compost to spread over the potato bed in spring you do not want to have to barrow the stuff from the other end of the plot. Instead, the heap is made right next to where it is to be used. The heap is made in the usual way (see p. 20) but the base is larger, being 3·5 × 3·5 m (12 × 12 ft). As wastes are added periodically, so a large sheet of 500-gauge black polythene is draped over them and weighed down. When the heap has been completed old sacks, rugs or carpets are placed on its top and sides. The polythene sheet is then draped over the heap and secured in position with scrap iron poles. Criticism of the Black Sheet method can come from theorists who have not tried it, that insufficient air reaches the wastes during the initial fermentation. Although the base of the sheet is anchored to the soil by the scrap iron poles or other weighty objects, plenty of air does reach the wastes. On a windy day air passing upwards may be seen moving the polythene sheeting.

Various special methods of constructing compost heaps have been worked out by specialists. By all means follow these special methods if you already practise compost-making by one of them. Larger heaps ferment and decompose more quickly than small heaps. A smallish heap will decompose more rapidly if protected by a container – that is, a box. The box may be of any material to hand but a treated wooden slatted box is considered ideal. Asbestos, tinplate, bricks, concrete or railway sleepers are other materials for box construction. A solid-sided container may prevent adequate air from reaching the wastes. It would be wise, therefore, using a crow bar of a stout pole or post, to make a hole from top to bottom of such heaps to admit more air.

Before a compost heap is started the soil where the heap is to be made should be dug over to a depth of two or three inches and all weeds and their roots removed. Ideally heaps should be made in layers. In practice this is rarely possible. Any rather large woody items make a good base if they are to hand. If I have any cabbage, Brussels sprouts or broccoli stumps, I use them as the base of a heap. This rough base is not essential. The first and subsequent layers of the heap can consist of any wastes to hand. If wastes come in as dribs and drabs, add them as they are to hand, covering them with a little soil. Each layer can be 30 cm (1 ft) or so thick. Never have a whole layer of only sappy cut grass and weeds or of lawn mowings. This kind of stuff compacts and changes to smelly silage. All wastes should be moist. Paper and cardboard need soaking; leaving it out in heavy rain can do the trick. Animal manure may be spread lightly over layers or added in small quantities now and then. A few shovels of garden top soil should be spread over each layer, too. The top soil weighs down the wastes and introduces fungi and bacteria to the heap. Lime may be sprinkled on to each soil addition. Wood ashes from an indoor fire or from a bonfire may be used instead of lime. This is of particular value where the garden soil is on the acid side.

The final height of the heap will vary, depending on the height of the 'box'. Black Sheet heaps may be 1·8 m (6 ft) high when completed. It is impossible to keep the sides at an angle of 90°. A heap started with a base 3·5 × 3·5 m (12 × 12 ft) will have top dimensions of no more than 90 × 90 cm (3 × 3 ft) when the heap is from 1·5–1·8 m (5–6 ft) high. The retention of engendered heat within the heap is assisted in the Black Sheet method by covering the heap immediately after any wastes have been added and, of course, on its completion. Compost in containers may be protected by having wooden, metal or asbestos lids or by simply covering the surface of the wastes and of the completed heap with a sheet of black polythene. As I have said, speed in making garden compost is important. Nobody wants heaps standing around the garden for a year or two although far too many gardeners put up with this sort of thing. After completion a heap should be ready within from five to six weeks if the heap were made in spring or summer; autumn-made heaps take longer and may not heat up well. In winter there are relatively few wastes around; never sufficient for the making of a complete heap. I like to keep winter wastes aside and include them in a large heap made in April. The inclusion of so-called activators is not necessary where small quantities of animal dung are used. Where no animal wastes are available, a herbal activator or dried blood may possibly be useful. For goodness' sake don't take the advice so often given that a compost heap should be turned after the first fermentation has almost spent itself. I have turned so many compost heaps in my time and it was dreadfully hard, smelly work! I am quite sure I wasted time and energy in doing so and have given it up. True, an unturned heap (especially a heap made by the Black Sheet method) may have an exterior 2·5 cm (1 in) or so of undecomposed wastes, which may be sliced off, if one so wishes, and incorporated in the new heap one is starting. Do not worry about partial decomposition. Where garden compost is being spread as a mulch, any partially decomposed wastes will almost certainly disintegrate quite rapidly. The compost you spread over the potato bed in April may appear pretty rough but when digging the crop you will find the rough stuff has decomposed pretty well.

Always use garden compost generously. In the reclamation of a garden or allotment a large barrowload per square metre or yard is about the right quantity to spread over dug soil. The digging in of garden compost is helpful in lightening heavy soils and in improving the water-holding capacity of light soils. With the several light soils I have had to improve I have simply spread garden compost in the form of a thick mulch (surface cover). Worms and other friendly soil inhabitants mix the compost mulch into the topsoil. I mix it in, too, when cultivating during the summer and during annual digging.

Those who are not in favour of gardening on the cheap and sprinkle a bit of this and that from the chemist's bag plus a modicum of shop-bought peat, warn the gardener that home-made, cost-free compost contains weed seeds. It does. Many are destroyed when a heap ferments well and at a high temperature but some thousands always remain viable. On top of that, the more fertile you make your own soil, the more likely weed seeds blown on to it will germinate freely. But dealing with weed seedlings is not all that difficult if you use your fingers, a hand fork and one or more garden hoes. In this book I have frequently re-commended the use of good propagating mediums like Levington Potting Compost for raising of seedlings. This proprietary compost is weed free. Providing you can recognize the seed leaves of your vegetables and take prompt action when the first flush of weed seedlings appear, you can economize by making do with sifted garden compost instead of proprietary seed or potting composts. I used sifted garden compost on the grand scale when raising large quantites of cabbage, lettuce, tomato and marrow plants for sale. The use of the home-made product reduced my costs enormously. It should never be partially sterilized by the use of heat, boiling water or a chemical.

Other organically-based manures

Manures based on composted animal manures or industrial wastes are around; they have to be bought. Spent mushroom compost is also available. It should be well decomposed and will possibly contain lime in some form or other. Mushroom composts may, however, also contain residues of chemical pesticides.

Green manures

These are plants which the gardener may grow himself in soil which is not occupied by food crops. Typical green manures are agricultural lupins, tic and daffa beans, rye grass and mustard. It is rare for any part of the garden or allotment to be vacant during the summer season. During October parts will, however, be ready for tidying up and I suggest the sowing of tic or daffa beans then. Sow seeds at a depth of 2·5–5 cm (1–2 ins) as closely as you wish. These field beans are closely related to our garden broad beans. Being legumes, their roots have nitrogen nodules. Dig or hoe in plants with their valuable roots during March. Potatoes or any brassicas may be grown where these legumes were mixed into the soil. This operation is very much worth while if your soil is light (sandy) and you prefer to dig it in early autumn rather than wait until the spring. The green manure plants will make use of plant nutrients in the top soil and prevent their being leached (washed down) into the subsoil. If you are moving house and have no time to continue sowing and planting for summer and autumn, sow agricultural lupins or mustard in spring. Here again sow thickly. Pull up all of the plants before they come into flower and take them to your new garden to start a compost heap there.

Fertilizers

These have to be bought and they are quite unnecessary if your garden or allotment soil is suitably fertile for food crops. A heavy-handed dose of chemical fertilizers can result in an acidic soil condition. Fertilizers can be helpful when growing plants in containers or if you have no home-made liquid manure with which to boost the growth of a special subject.

Herbicides and pesticides

Weed killers have no place at all in the kitchen garden or on the allotment. Apart from any poison hazard, there is the danger of explosion or of damage to plants on neighbouring allotments.

Pesticides should seldom be used. The appearance of aphids (black fly) on broad beans certainly warrants the use of a pesticide at once but the gnawing of a few unwanted, outer leaves of your brassicas (members of the cabbage family) does not call for chemical warfare on your part. Here and there in this book you will find references to some pests and there are suggestions on how to prevent them from appearing and how to deal with them if they do appear. Always use pesticides that are non-poisonous to man, his pets and to wildlife. Derris is a typical non-poisonous pesticide, but it is deadly to pool fish.

Tools

Basic tools for growing food crops are a garden fork, a spade, a hand fork, a garden trowel, a draw hoe and a Dutch hoe. An onion hoe is extremely useful to rid closely grown food plants of young weed growth; a spade is necessary for planting most fruits and for digging heavy (clay) soil.

Other equipment

Do not go on a spending spree if you are starting to grow food crops for the first time. Buy as and when the cultivation of a specific crop calls for additional equipment. Flower pots come in clay, plastic, whalehide (no connection with whales), polythene, card, paper and peat. Clay and plastic pots have a potentially long life. A garden frame is helpful for raising seedlings in spring, for summer crops of some less hardy vegetables, for over-wintering vegetable seedlings and for ripening off onions and shallots in a wet season. Perhaps you can make your own cheaply? I made a couple of dozen large, movable frames years ago. The first lot was made from scrap angle iron salvaged from old bedsteads and lightweight angle iron. But do not be bound by my ideas. Study garden frames in shops and in neighbours' gardens and design your own cheaply. My first 'garden frame' was simply several pieces of glass taken out of ancient picture frames and pushed into dug soil, with other sheets laid on top to form a 'roof'. I grew an excellent crop of melons in that 'frame'.

Most garden frames stand in the same position in the garden; cloches are always moved around. Glass cloches are, I think, by

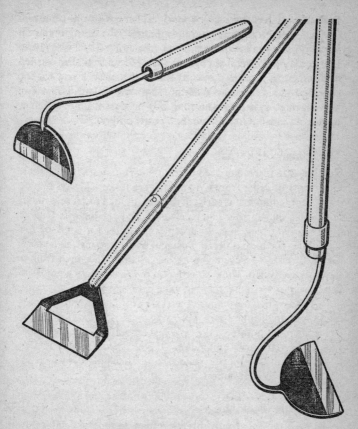

far the best and I particularly like the Low Barn pattern. Plastic cloches can become brittle and the newer polythene tunnel cloches do not remain securely positioned in my very sandy soil. But do not let me put you off the cheaper plastic or polythene kinds. Try one or two and come to your own conclusions. Here, again, why not design and construct your own particular cloches to suit your needs? I grew all kinds of fruits and vegetables before I had a greenhouse. Now, of course, I have got so used to having one that I find it well nigh indispensable. But please do not think that to produce a very wide selection of food crops you just must go out and spend a fortune on a greenhouse. Two of my mates on our allotment site have greenhouses, measuring 3 × 1·8 m (10 × 6 ft) and each greenhouse cost less than £5. Scrap timber rescued from a factory bonfire was used for the framework and for the door and lights (windows). Clear 150-gauge polythene film was the 'glazing' material. The film will need replacing within a couple of years but this will not be a costly outlay.

The annual seed order

You can buy vegetable seeds, seed potatoes, onion sets and shallots locally or order from a mail order seedsman. Always buy or order your requirements early; in the case of mail order seedsmen, this means shortly after you receive the seed catalogue in winter, otherwise you may have to accept substitutes for some of the specialities you have ordered. Postage costs are so high these days that I suggest you buy seed potatoes locally rather than from a far-away seedsman. The seed order on p. 174 is simply a guide. If you have just started gardening, take care that you do not over-buy. A chat with a neighbour or a fellow plot-holder may be helpful in gauging what room you may have for various crops. Remember that potatoes take up a vast amount of room but need very little as regards cultivation. If you spend most summer weekends at the seaside, then choose crops like potatoes which do not call for regular attention.

Fruit versus vegetables

Fruits need far less regular attention than do most vegetables. It would not be wise to plant tree fruits on an allotment (regulations often prevent the planting of trees and you are inviting thieves) but two or more garden apple trees should lead to fine crops with the minimum amount of work on your part. Any soft fruit is worth growing for eating fresh, jams, bottling, freezing or for dessert use in its season. I find it is not stolen as is the fruit from trees on an allotment. I particularly recommend raspberries for garden or allotment growing, if you are looking for a crop which calls for little time and work from you. Trained blackberries are also worth growing. Here, again, little work has to be expended and returns are excellent.

The question of water

In Chapter 1 I mention the importance of a water supply for allotment crops. Watering garden-grown food crops is not a great problem providing any regulations concerning the water supply are fulfilled. Gardeners in many parts of Britain do not have to water fruit and vegetables all that regularly in late spring and summer. In the drier eastern half of England, water can often make the difference between first-class crops and no crops at all. Get to know when water ought to be applied. When going away for summer holidays, arrange with a neighbour or a fellow plot-holder to water your greenhouse-, cloche- or frame-grown vegetables. In the garden itself, mulches help a lot in the retention of soil moisture in dry summer weather and suppress weed seedlings. Straw and lawn mowings are excellent mulches. These soil covers should not be laid down until the soil has warmed up in late spring or early summer.

Cooperation between gardeners

Get to know what your neighbours or fellow plot-holders are growing. Foster sharing. You are bound to have a surplus of plants and produce now and then which can be shared. It is of great help to gardeners and plot-holders if camaraderie exists. I am certainly most grateful to my own neighbours and mates on the allotment site for plants and produce when I am short.

Children and teenagers

They are the gardeners (or possibly the vandals) of tomorrow. A child or teenager with respect or interest in gardening has no respect for vandals and hates vandalism. I am absolutely against putting a child or teenager to work in the garden. Only if the boy or girl wants to help should this be encouraged. It amazes me just what a youngster from a tower-block home can do – and just for the fun of it. These kids, without even a flowerpot of soil in the home, can really enjoy themselves picking (and sampling) fruit, watering, building a compost heap, cleaning the garden pool or tidying up the garden shed. Local kids should be encouraged in the garden and on allotment sites. We have a duty to introduce them to the exciting and rewarding hobby of gardening.

Home freezing

Throughout this book you will come across references to the freezing of various home-grown produce. If you have a freezer you will already appreciate its great value as a store of good things, particularly when you can enjoy summer specialities in the depths of winter. If you have no freezer yet, I do suggest that you think about investing in one. I note with satisfaction that some specialist writers on home-freezing tell their readers that only home-grown produce is worth freezer space. Only the home food grower can harvest just at the right time and then hurry the produce through any freezing technique and into the freezer itself. For the plot-holder with a home halfway to heaven or living in a gardenless maisonette, a home freezer is the answer to some storage problems.

Learning from others

Watching how other gardeners do garden work is helpful but not all of them (even the old hands) are as knowledgeable as the beginner may think. Gardening cannot be learnt from this book or from any other book. Specialist writers can only guide you. When I started fruit and vegetable growing I found information in books at the public library. Only after reading several books did I buy one or two which seemed to fit in with my requirements. Some books for further reading are suggested in Appendix 1. Then there are the gardening magazines, listed in the same place (see p. 170). If you do not already take one of them regularly, buy a sample copy of each of them or look through them at your local public library. Would the regular arrival of a copy of one of them help you in your search for knowledge as a gardener? If you think as I do, you will place an order and enjoy your gardening weekly or monthly. Radio and television gardening programmes are helpful, too, but they are usually so quick and brief. Still, you are bound to pick up some tips from them.

3 Vegetables to grow and enjoy

Chinese artichoke

Not a commonly-grown vegetable but raised for its small, cork-screw-like tubers. Choose a sunny position and plant single tubers at 30 cm (1 ft) apart in March or early April. The soil should be reasonably fertile and preferably have been dressed with garden compost for a different crop in the previous season. A cabbage dibber may be used to make 10-cm (4-in) deep planting holes into which tubers can be dropped. After planting, fill the holes with soil. If you are growing more than one row, leave 35 cm (15 in) between rows. Hoe occasionally between the rows to keep down weeds but do not use a hoe or hand fork near the plants, otherwise the roots and tubers may be damaged. Pull up weeds near the plants, which is not difficult when the soil is moist. Give water in dry summer spells. No other cultivation is necessary. The plants attain a height of about 30 cm (1 ft) and resemble the weed, Dead Nettle. Flower stems are sometimes made; the flowers are inconspicuous. The plants die in late autumn when tubers are ready for digging. Dig roots as and when wanted until February. If not used quickly the tubers become brown. When digging the last roots, set aside tubers for replanting elsewhere in the garden. Chinese artichokes have to be washed and scrubbed well before they are cooked; they cannot be peeled. I bought tubers at a Soho greengrocer and have had supplies ever since. There is no British supplier of tubers as yet, although Dobies are considering growing them from my stock.

Globe artichoke

This is the true artichoke. The plant resembles a thistle, with large leaves and buds. If permitted to flower it has large mauve/purple blooms, rarely seen because this vegetable is grown for its edible flower buds. Choose a sunny position and set out young plants of a named variety such as Vert de Laon in April. The soil should be fertile and each plant should be at 90 cm–1·2 m (3–4 ft) from its neighbour. Two or four plants are usually grown. After planting spread a mulch of garden compost around the plants and water in dry weather. Attend to any necessary weeding but use a hand fork rather than a hoe. Expect only a few buds in the first summer but more in the next three. After the fourth summer it is usual to dig up the plants and to start afresh by planting strong sucker plants with roots cut from the old plants with a sharp knife. To have large buds, pinch off smaller ones around the main bud before they are 2·5 cm (1 in) in diameter. The buds *must* be fully developed but still quite tight before they are cut. If too many buds are ready for use, cut them with 15 cm (6 ins) of stem and stand them in a jar of water in a cool place. The buds may also be blanched and frozen. After all the buds have been harvested, cut off the flowering stems and chop them in pieces for the compost heap. In late autumn or early winter tidy up the bed by removing dying and dead foliage. In very cold parts of the country the spreading of sifted ash quite thickly over the crowns of the plants is advised after the bed has been tidied up. The ash must be removed in March and replaced with a mulch of garden compost.

Jerusalem artichoke

Grown for its tubers. Their flavour is liked by some; others say they have a 'smoky' taste. There are red- and white-skinned forms and they resemble small, knobbly potatoes. As with potatoes, one starts off with tubers, planted as and when the soil is workable between January and early April. Although the plants will grow in almost any sort of soil, cropping at the rate of about 2 kgs (5 lb) per root cannot be expected unless the soil is sufficiently fertile. Because the plants can reach a height of 2·5 m (8 ft), care should be taken so that they are not grown where they will shade other vegetables. Planting holes 10–15 cm (4–6 ins) deep and 30 cm (12 ins) apart may be made with a trowel or with a cabbage dibber. Mulching the bed after planting with garden compost ensures that the plants will have adequate nourishment. Keep down weeds and in late autumn cut back the stems to about

30 cm (1 ft) high. Roots are ready for digging when wanted between November and late February. The tubers do not store well but may be boiled and served with a cheese sauce or cooked, mashed and frozen for use in soups. When digging, make sure that every tuber is removed from the soil and choose a few of the larger tubers to replant immediately, elsewhere in the garden for next winter's supplies. Any left in the ground will grow up like weeds in the following spring.

Asparagus

Seldom seen in gardens or on allotments because of the large amount of space a bed requires. The tender shoots for which asparagus is grown appear here and there over a period of almost two months. To have sufficient shoots at any one time you will need two or three dozen plants. A sunny aspect should be chosen for the bed but not a place where very strong winds will damage the tall summer growth. The soil must drain well and if clay is known to exist beneath the top soil, it should be broken into with a spade and rubble and gritty sand mixed with it in the subsoil so that drainage is really good. Where the topsoil itself is heavy with a high clay content, it would be better to have a raised bed for asparagus. Do this by digging soil from around the bed and piling it 15–20 cm (6–8 ins) above the surrounding ground. An asparagus bed has a potential life of about twenty years so that during the preparation of the bed well-rotted manure or garden compost should be incorporated generously into the soil. If there is any leaf mould to hand this, too, may be mixed into the soil. If you have recently taken over a very weedy garden or allotment, do not consider making an asparagus bed until you have got rid of roots of perennial weeds like bindweed, creeping thistle and goutweed. A bed 1·5 m (5 ft) wide will take two rows of plants at almost 60 cm (2 ft) apart and the plants at 45 cm (18 ins) apart in the rows. Although asparagus plants may be raised from seed, it is easier to start off with two-year-old plants because no shoots may be cut from asparagus until the plants are four years old and few gardeners wish to wait that long. Late March and early April are the correct planting times. Order male plants and as soon as your plants arrive from the nurseryman, get them planted. The roots must never be allowed to get dry. To plant take out 22-cm (9-ins) deep furrows, using a spade or draw hoe. Make a slight mound at the bottom of the furrows and spread the spidery roots of the asparagus plants over the mounds. Fill in the furrows with soil and if the ground is not wet, water well. Keep the bed free from annual weeds and water in dry summer weather. Provide the top growth with supports such as stout bamboo canes. In November each year, the top (the asparagus 'fern') will be yellow, and should be cut back to within 2·5 cm (1 in) of the ground. Clear away any debris and spread well-rotted dung or garden compost thickly all over the bed. Asparagus plants make roots near the surface of the ground so that any cultivation must be shallow. Female plants have berries; if some of the plants turn out to be female, pick off the berries or they will fall and you will probably have asparagus seedlings like weeds all over the bed. When your plants are four years old, start cutting the succulent shoots when they are about 10 cm (4 ins) tall in late April. Cut the shoots well below soil level, using a sharp knife. Stop cutting shoots in mid June and allow natural top growth to grow. If the foliage is being eaten, look for small black and orange beetles. Pick them off.

Asparagus pea

Not a true pea and because of the rectangular shape of the edible pods, it is sometimes called the 'winged pea'. Choose a sunny spot and sow during early May and in 2·5–5 cm (1–2 ins) seed drills. Space the seeds at 20 cm (8 ins) apart and in a double, staggered row. In colder parts seeds should be sown in small pots in a greenhouse or garden frame in early May and the plants set out in the garden a month later. Seed may also be sown under cloches in early May. The plants grow to a height of about 30 cm (1 ft) and have brick-red, pea-like flowers. Under the weight of the crop, the plants tend to topple over; this can be prevented by pushing twiggy brushwood on either side of the row or by supporting the plants with strings tied to short canes. Use the hoe to keep down weeds and water in dry weather. Pick the pods when they are less than 2·5 cm (1 in) long. Longer pods are 'stringy' and unpalatable. Cropping continues for several weeks.

Aubergine

Also known as 'Egg Plant', is grown for the purple fruits. The aubergine plant is tender and best grown in a slightly heated greenhouse. Sow seeds in small flowerpots at a temperature of from 60–65°F (16–19°C) in March. Sow two seeds in each pot and pinch off the second weaker seedling. A month or so later set out the plants in the greenhouse border 45 cm (18 ins) apart. The soil in the border should have been enriched with garden compost – either dug in or simply spread on as a 2·5–5 cm (1–2 in) mulch. For economy of precious greenhouse space, aubergine seedlings may be potted on into 15-cm (6-in) diameter pots, stood on the greenhouse staging. In the pots I use a mixture of good top soil and garden compost. When the plants are between 15 and 22 cm (6 and 9 ins) tall, pinch out the central growing point at the top of the plants to encourage branching. Keep the plants well supplied with water. Pot plants benefit from liquid manure or fertilizer feeds when fruits are swelling. Discontinue feeding when the fruits are full size. Cut the fruits when they have a polished appearance and are well-coloured.

Broad beans

There are white, green and red-seeded forms. The site for the crop should be as open as possible and an allotment is just the place. It should be land dressed rather heavily for a different vegetable in the previous season. This means that broad beans may be grown where potatoes, winter greens or cauliflower were grown. The soil should drain well but should not dry out rapidly in summer. A very early start may be made by sowing in November but if winters are usually severe where you live, be prepared to lose all or most of the seedlings. Protecting the seed row with cloches can prevent this but in a mild winter cloches should be removed, otherwise the seedlings can outgrow the height of them during February and they simply have to be removed then. Then in March a very cold spell may occur and ruin the tender, tall plants. Aquadulce is the variety for an autumn sowing and is also the broad bean for sowing with cloche protection in January. For February and March sowings, either with or without cloche protection, there is a good choice of varieties and I suggest Imperial

Green Longpod and Masterpiece Green Longpod. These may also be sown in April if you have a soil which never permits you to start your seed sowings earlier. For April sowing you may also like to try Giant Four Seeded White Windsor. The Sutton is in a class of its own. This very dwarf plant is not only ideal for cloche work but a boon to those whose garden is in a veritable wind tunnel and where tall-growing sorts of broad beans suffer badly from winds. Seeds may also be sown in an unheated greenhouse or frame in January or February. Sow one seed in each 9 cm ($3\frac{1}{2}$ in) pot. Set the plants outdoors in early April. If the weather is very cold, it is wise to give the row of seedlings cloche protection. To sow broad beans in the garden make a 5 cm (2 in) deep furrow with a draw hoe. Sow seeds at 15–20 cm (6–8 ins) apart in a double, staggered row. A half-pint packet is sufficient for a double row of about 6 metres (20 ft) Sow a few extra seeds at the end of the row to fill in any gaps. Use a rake or your boots to draw soil over the furrow to fill it in. If you are sowing another row alongside leave a distance of 75 cm ($2\frac{1}{2}$ ft). Label the row. If you are using cloches set them in position, but they must be taken off before the plants reach the top of them. Hoe around the plants regularly and pull up any weeds which germinate among the plants. If you fear that strong winds may blow down tall growers, give the plants some supports. I use a few strong canes linked together with string. Broad bean plants attract Black Bean aphis. If this pest is not prevented or defeated, the plants can be ruined. The aphids may then continue their nasty work on dwarf and runner beans in your garden and in your neighbours', and on some allotment sites the growing of broad beans is not allowed because of the danger of aphis spreading from allotment to allotment. Earlier sowings lead to plants which are not so attractive to the pest when it starts looking for broad beans in May. Preventive measures to take against aphids are (a) spray plants regularly with liquid derris during May; (b) pinch off the top of the plants as soon as the first flowers on the plants are setting tiny pods; (c) tear off any young growths which appear at the base of the plants. If aphids get a firm foothold, non-toxic (to us) sprays are not always effective. If you use more potent sprays or dusts, take care that they do not harm you or your family. Nicotine, for example, is poisonous. Remember, too, that ladybirds will almost certainly be present and will be devouring the aphids and that honey bees and wild bees will be visiting the plants during flowering. Give the plants plenty of water in dry summer weather and pick the pods when they are plump but before the seeds become old and 'leathery'. This is a first-class vegetable for home freezing and where there is room a special row should be grown for this purpose.

Dwarf French beans

Grown for two different reasons. The plants invariably come into bearing before scarlet runners and this is the favourite bean for home freezing. The plants are compact bushes and cropping is spread over a month at least. Older varieties like Canadian Wonder tend to have a 'string' running the length of the pod if not picked in their prime. This 'string' has to be removed by the cook. Newer varieties such as Glamis do not have this. Most dwarf bean varieties bear green pods; there are, however, yellow-podded ones (such as Cherokee Wax) and purple-podded sorts (such as Royalty). The pods of the yellows and purples are quite stringless. The purple coloration changes to bright green during cooking. Glamis has the reputation of being able to stand up to lower temperatures than most other dwarf beans.

In the crop rotation French beans can be sown where brussels sprouts and other members of the cabbage tribe were grown in the previous season. The site itself should be a sunny one but not exposed to strong, cold winds. Ideally, the soil should be light and well drained. Seeds may be sown in pots in a greenhouse or garden frame during April for plants to set out in the garden (preferably with cloche protection) in May. It is more usual to wait until late April or early May and to sow seeds in the ground in exactly the same way as broad beans. If the ground is dry, flood the flat-bottomed drill with water and sow when this has drained away. If you are making more than one row space the rows at 1·2 metres (4 ft) apart.

Cultivation consists of hoeing periodically to keep down weeds, hand weeding (when necessary) among the plants and watering well in dry weather in July and August. If you want green beans for freezing, sow a row especially for this purpose. As there is no hurry for the beans, wait until late May before sowing. If your plants tend to topple soil-wards under the weight of crop push a few short bamboo canes on either side of the rows. Link the canes with one or two lengths of string. Do not use tall canes; if you do you may damage one of your eyes when bending down to pick the crop. Black Bean aphis is seldom a worry on dwarf beans. First pods from an April sowing will be ready for use during the last half of July. Go over the plants two or three times a week and pick every young pod of reasonable length. Never allow a pod to swell its seeds. Where this happens, the plant bearing the pod just stops producing more pods. For more French beans in September and October sow again in June and July. There are also climbing sorts of french beans.

Runner beans

This is Britain's favourite summer vegetable. Often called the 'scarlet runner' although there are also white, white and red as well as pink-flowerers. To add to the confusion there are dwarf sorts – Hammond's Dwarf Scarlet, Hammond's Dwarf White. These two are sown and cultivated in exactly the same manner as dwarf French beans. Runner bean seeds may be sown in pots or trays in late April or early May in a greenhouse or frame for plants to set out in the garden during early June. If you are going to sow directly in the garden soil – and this is the more usual way – wait until some time in May. If you live in the south and wish to take a chance by sowing in April, by all means do so. Very many gardeners do. When they are lucky they are picking runner beans several weeks earlier than their neighbours. When they are unlucky and have the seedlings blackened by a late May frost, they have to start all over again. The exhibitor goes to enormous trouble in preparing the bed where runner seeds are to be sown. For the home food grower all that is needed is fertile soil which has been dug over and from which weeds and their roots have been removed. The soil must be fertile, drain well and not be acidic. Scarlet-flowered varieties are preferred by most gardeners and for cropping and length of pod I can recommend Enorma and

Prizetaker. Fry and Desirée are new, white-flowered runners. The pods are not all that long but they are stringless.

There are two ways of growing runner beans – on supports or on the flat. For straight, long pods supports are necessary. These can be traditional bean poles erected to form an inverted 'V' structure, metal or plastic mesh, bean nets (particularly as supplied with rust-free supports by Agriframes, East Grinstead, Sussex) or a wire mesh garden fence. This can be heightened to 1·8 m (6 ft) with some stout poles and a roll of 'Weldmesh' or 'Netlon'

plastic mesh. Sow the seeds in a 5-cm (2-in) deep, narrow furrow. Space the seeds 15–20 cm (6–8 ins) apart and sow a few extra seeds at the end of the row so that you will have spare seedlings to fill any gaps. Set out pot or box-raised seedlings at the same distances. The plants will twine around and climb the supports. When the plants reach the top, pinch off the growing point of each plant. The other way of growing runners is a method adopted by gardeners living in such windy spots that strong winds ruin the foliage and flowers of runner plants on supports. The seeds are sown in a flat-bottomed, 22-cm (9-in) wide furrow in exactly the same way as are broad and dwarf beans. When the plants are about 30 cm (12 ins) high, the growing point at the top of each waving stem is pinched back by 5 cm (2 ins). Branching side stems then form. These, too, are pinched back by 5 cm (2 ins) when they are about 45 cm (18 ins) long. As and when more branching shoots are made, these too are nipped back. Finally one has a row of low bushes. For this method a shorter-podded runner like Kelvedon Marvel or Fry is chosen.

Runner plants need plenty of water in dry weather. If you fear an attack (or see any on the plants) of Black Bean aphis, spray with liquid derris or a proprietary, non-toxic insecticide. Always spray in the evening so that bees are not harmed. If ladybirds are on the plants, these natural pest-killers may clear up the trouble for you. Harvest runner beans when they are quite flat and young. At this stage no runner beans have the objectionable string, so often a feature of shop-bought pods. Your garden-grown pods will just need topping and tailing before being sliced for immediate use or for freezing. Never allow a pod to swell its seeds. If you do, cropping will stop from that plant. If you are going on holiday for a week or so, ask a neighbour to pick your runner beans regularly. If you wish to save your own seeds, mark a few plants and do not pick any of the pods when they are fresh and green. Leave them all to swell seeds and to become dry and brown; then pick and shell the pods in autumn.

Beetroot

Long-rooted beets are no longer popular; round and tankard-shaped beets are preferred. In recent years golden and white-fleshed beets have been introduced but for salads most of us continue to grow ones with deep red flesh. Detroit and Boltardy are round varieties; Formanova and Cylindra (Housewives' Choice) are tankard-shaped. Boltardy is deservedly popular because the seedlings are unlikely to 'bolt' when sown in soils with low temperatures. Choose a spot in the garden which received manure or garden compost for a different crop last year. Rake the dug soil well and remove any large stones. A sowing may be made in early April in the south; later that month in other parts unless cloche protection is to be given. Sowings may also be made in May, June or July. Make 2·5-cm (1-in) deep seed drills at 30 cm (12 ins) apart and sprinkle the seeds fairly thinly in them, as each seed is actually a cluster of seeds. Use a rake or your boots to scuffle soil back into the furrows and label the rows. As soon as the seedlings show, start your war on weeds by hoeing (the Dutch hoe is the best tool) between the rows. If your seedlings are beneath cloches, pay attention to any necessary watering. Remove the cloches as soon as the weather warms up. A late spring frost is not likely to harm beet seedlings. Where seedlings look far too tightly packed, thin them so that you are left with plants at about 7·5 cm (3 in) apart. Pull beets for summer salads when they are small; you can start when they are of golfball size. Those which are left will grow larger. Remember, it's young beets which have the best flavour. Give beet plants a good soaking in dry weather. The traditional way of storing beets is to harvest in early October, twist off the foliage and store, sandwich fashion, in boxes of dry ashes or peat. Put the boxes in an outhouse, dry shed or garage. I find it simpler to harvest in July or August and to boil the beets before slicing them and bottling in vinegar. You may home-freeze your beets when they are small and tastier. Boil the beets until they are tender. Then peel, slice or dice and cool well before packing into bags or cartons for the freezer.

Brassicas

In gardening jargon this term covers all members of the cabbage family – broccoli, brussels sprouts, cabbages, cauliflower, kale. For summer, autumn and winter supplies, seeds of all of them are sown in spring. The easiest way of going about the job is to wait until the soil is warming up in mid April and to choose a sunny spot for the seed bed, where animal manure has not been dug in. If the soil was not dug within the last few weeks, fork it over to a depth of from 15–20 cm (6–8 ins). Remove any weeds and roots. Rake level and firm gently with your boots. Rake level again. If you feel the soil is not as fertile as it ought to be you can spread on it a 2·5-cm (1-in) mulch of sifted garden compost or Levington Potting Compost. Make 2·5-cm (1-in) deep narrow furrows at 20 cm (8 ins) apart. If the ground is dry, fill the furrows with water. Have your labels ready and sow seeds pretty thickly when the water has drained away. Fill the furrows and firm gently. Keep the bed moist (using a rose on the can or a sprinkler system) if the weather stays dry both before and after germination takes place. Keep down weeds and for stronger, sturdier young plants dig up the lot in mid May and replant the best of them in the same seed bed or elsewhere, using a cabbage dibber or a short bamboo cane to make the planting holes (see Table, p. 44). Water well after planting. Although the young plants are set at no more than 2·5 cm (1 in) or so apart in the nursery bed, the extra room they have really does lead to stronger plants within from two to three weeks. The transplanting to a nursery bed need not be carried out with seedlings of early summer cabbage. They make rapid growth in the seed bed and when you are moving all other seedlings to the nursery bed, the cabbage seedlings will possibly be at just the right stage (with four or five 'true' (cabbage-like) leaves for planting out where they are to grow.

The ground where brassicas are to be grown should preferably have been dug a month or so before planting out takes place. If you have to set out plants in recently dug soil, firm it well. This simply means walking all over it and then raking it level. Brassicas are greedy feeders and to ensure that I obtain the finest possible results, I provide my plants with all the nourishment they may need by spreading a 2·5-cm (1-in) thick mulch of garden compost over the entire bed when the ground is moist. The compost mulch is also linked with the defeat of Cabbage Root Fly damage – see p. 44. Use a garden line to have straight rows; the cabbage dibber is the correct tool for the planting of brassicas. If rain has not fallen within a day or two, soak the bed of brassica seedlings on the evening before you intend to move them to their growing positions. When pulling the seedlings out of the ground, hold them at the base of the stem, not by the leaves. Most brassicas need quite a lot of room for good development.

Make the planting holes. Fill them with water if the soil is dry. Allow the water to drain away. Then plant so that the lowest leaf of each plant is just above the level of the surrounding soil. Firm around each plant with the dibber. You can check if you have planted quite firmly by giving a gentle tug at a leaf. The plant

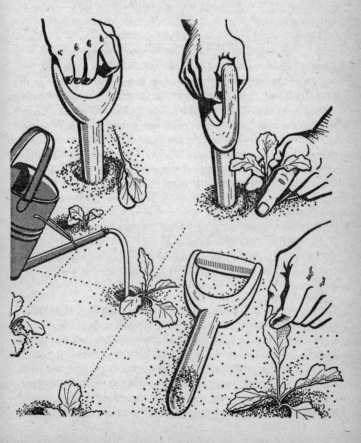

Planting distances for brassicas

	Between rows		Between plants in the rows	
	cm	inches	cm	inches
Brussels sprouts	75	30	75	30
Cabbage summer	37–45	15–18	37–45	15–18
autumn, winter	60	24	45–60	18–24
spring	60	24	37–45	15–18
Cauliflower	60	24	45–50	18–20
Sprouting broccoli and kale	60	24	45–60	18–24

should remain in the soil. Unless the ground is quite wet I invariably pour water into the dibber holes. In dry weather the plants wilt badly and it is necessary to water again on the following day. A week later use the Dutch hoe to loosen any soil compacted around the plants and to prevent weeds from taking hold around them. Take care when hoeing that you do not stab the brassica plants and do not use this tool deeply. If you grow your brassicas in a mulch of garden compost there is little likelihood of much weed growth and your work as regards cultivation will be minimal. True, weeds will germinate but if the weather is very warm, the small seedlings will die.

Pests and diseases of brassicas

You may grow brassicas for years and never have any trouble with pests and diseases, but here are those you may have to deal with.

Cabbage Root Fly You are not likely to see these flies. The females are attracted to young brassicas by their smell. This odour appears to be greater after a batch of transplants has been set out in late May and June. Eggs are laid alongside the plants and the grubs tunnel into the roots and the below-ground part of the stem. The plants sicken and may die. When pulled up the white maggots may usually be seen on the roots. The simplest preventive measure is to set out transplants firmly. Firm soil prevents eggs from being laid in their correct place – just below the soil surface. If a mulch of garden compost is spread over the bed when transplants are being set out, the smell of the compost masks the odour emitted by the young brassicas.

Cabbage aphis Also known as Mealy aphis. These are greyish in colour and suck sap from the leaves which then become distorted. Any small colonies of these aphids should be killed by squeezing the leaf between the finger and thumb. Occasionally a plant here and there becomes badly infested. Should this happen, pull up the plant and bury it inside the compost heap. Poor soil conditions, a lack of available plant food or a lack of water lead to weak, slow-growing brassicas, which are likely to be the victims of cabbage aphis. The aphids arrive on summer brassicas from old brassica stumps left around from the previous season. It pays, therefore, to dig up, chop up and add to the compost all brassica stumps as soon as the last greens have been picked from them in spring. Unfortunately, far too many brassica plants are left about on allotment sites where the plants may be seen flowering in spring. It is from these plants that our own brassicas are likely to be visited by cabbage aphids.

Cabbage caterpillars The caterpillars of cabbage white butterflies and of the cabbage moth eat the leaves of brassicas. The caterpillars hatch from eggs laid on the leaves. Some authorities recommend the gardener to hunt and destroy the eggs. I do not suggest this as the gardener is likely to destroy pupae of ichneumon wasps by mistake and the ichneumon wasp (commonly called ichneumon fly) is a good friend of the gardener. The female wasps lay their eggs under the skin of cabbage caterpillars. The caterpillars are devoured by the ichneumon grubs which emerge from the dead caterpillars and pupate on brassica foliage. The first small cabbage caterpillars may be met with on spring cabbages in June. It is then that the last of these cabbages is being cut for use and the caterpillars are not a nuisance. The next brood makes its appearance on summer cabbages in July. A salt-water solution sprayed on the plants when the cabbages are very small can kill some of them. I do this and I pick off any I notice afterwards. In August and September I go over my brassica plants periodically and I pick off any caterpillars. Often I just haven't time to do this job more than twice during the season and, although I see caterpillars browsing on my brassica foliage, the damage is usually confined to the outer leaves, which are discarded by the cook anyway. It is the slow-growing brassica plant which falls victim to caterpillar infestation and what a mess results! The leaves resemble lace-work and the heart of the cabbage is gnawed and covered with caterpillar excrement. Slow growth of brassicas in summer may be due to poor soil conditions, to Club Root disease or simply to a lack of water. It is up to the gardener to make sure that his brassicas enjoy conditions which lead to even, good, strong growth.

Cabbage White Fly I had been growing brassicas for twenty-five years before I had seen this pest. It is only if you live in southern England that you are ever likely to see cabbage white flies and then only if we have one or two very mild winters. You will soon know if white flies are around. As you push alongside your tall leafy broccoli or bend down to cut a cabbage a vast host of what look like minute white moths fly around you in a cloud and settle quickly on brassicas, the soil and on you! Although the flies are sap suckers, they in no way weaken my healthy brassica plants. Fortunately the flies inhabit the outer leaves and do not enter the hearts of cabbages or brussels sprouts. If all brassicas are cut and soaked in salt water before being rinsed and cooked, there should be no danger of eating the flies.

Club Root This is the nastiest of all brassica troubles and a common one, especially on allotment sites where plot-holders have never bothered to garden correctly by rotating crops and by building up soil fertility. The disease is fungal. Its symptoms are a stunting or dwarfing of brassica plants which may also die. When the plants are pulled up there are large tumours on the roots. These give rise to the alternative name of 'Finger-and-Toe' for this disease. But things may be worse. The whole root system may be swollen and 'clubbed' and smell pretty nastily. Preventive measures against Club Root are: (a) always examine the roots of any brassica seedlings you buy or are given. Do not plant any which have knobbly swellings on the roots. Burn them. The

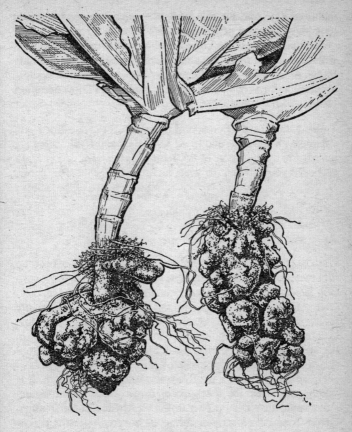

swellings may be due to other reasons and not to this nasty fungus but it pays to play safe; (*b*) always make your own brassica seed bed in soil which you know is not infected with the disease. Your garden soil may be 'clean' but the allotment soil infected. Grow your cabbage seedlings in the garden, not on the allotment; (*c*) if the soil drains badly do all you can to rectify this fault; (*d*) if a soil test shows that the soil is acidic, apply powdered chalk (lime) annually for two years at the rate of up to 500 grammes per sq m (2 lb per sq yd); (*e*) never use chemical fertilizers or raw animal manures; (*f*) build up soil fertility by applying regular, heavy dressings of mature garden compost.

Although the soil of a complete allotment site may be infected with Club Root fungus, the plot-holder who builds up soil fertility on his or her own plot will find that the disease will be a slight nuisance at times or will disappear completely. I know because I have had this trouble.

Turnip Gall Weevil Do not confuse swellings of Club Root with swellings on the stem and at or just below soil level. These are galls made by the larvae of the Turnip Gall Weevil. If you cut a gall open you will find the white larva curled inside. The Turnip Gall Weevil does not inconvenience healthy plants of the cabbage tribe and may be ignored.
See also Broccoli, Cabbage, Cauliflower, Kale

Broccoli

Until recently seedsmen and horticultural writers divided broccoli into two groups – heading and sprouting. It is now the practice to call heading broccoli 'winter cauliflowers' (see p. 56). This section therefore deals only with the sprouting forms. These are Green Sprouting (with alternative names Italian Sprouting, Calabrese), Purple Sprouting and White Sprouting. All are sown in the brassica seed bed during April. Stronger transplants are obtained if the seedlings are moved to a nursery bed (see Brassicas).

Green Sprouting is a relatively new vegetable to Britain. It is widely grown for the quick-freeze industry and books rightly recommend that it be grown in the garden for home freezing. Green Comet is an early-maturing variety for August and September. Late Corona provides a follow-on crop. If the winter is mild, cropping continues into January. The green central head may be cut and used as cauliflower. The plants then make thick side shoots for cutting when about 15 cm (6 ins) long and these are delicious when boiled. I remove the few leaves and peel the stems. Green Sprouting must have really fertile soil and sufficient moisture at the roots in a dry summer.

Purple and White Sprouting are very hardy brassicas and are grown for supplies of spring greens. In very mild winters there are shoots for use in January but the more usual time for harvesting is between late March and Spring Bank Holiday. When well grown, plants of Purple Sprouting are almost 90 cm (1 yd) high and a row of them looks like a thick hedge by March. White Sprouting has the reputation of being somewhat less hardy and is also a rather smaller plant. Both the Purple and the White stand up well to summer drought conditions and neither is likely to be harmed by Mealy aphis or by caterpillars. Both sorts are also far more tolerant of Club Root (see p. 46) than are cabbages, cauliflower or brussels sprouts. Pick shoots when the buds are white or creamy on White Sprouting and mauve/purple on Purple Sprouting. The length of the picked sprouts may be up to 20 cm (8 ins). After these have been culled, more, shorter shoots will follow and the very loose, central head may be cut, too. The flavour of White Sprouting is similar to cauliflower. Purple Sprouting is somewhat bitter. Country folk say the bitterness is due to its high iron content which, they add, means it is just the right, healthy vegetable for springtime. Never leave plants to flower. Pull or dig them up as soon as the last edible shoot has been picked, chop the stems into short sections and put them on the compost heap.

Brussels sprouts

We gardeners are apt to take things so much for granted and those of us who also write about our pet hobby so often assume that readers already know quite a bit about gardening. This attitude is wrong, as I found out some years ago when a fellow plot-holder asked if he might see my brussels sprouts plants. It was a shock to him (and a different sort of shock to me) to see that the sprouts formed in the leaf axils of the plants. He had expected to find his sprouts right at the top in a sort of 'nest'. True, he had spent his entire life in London and had only been able to garden when he had moved into the suburbs. As things turned out, he worked hard, quickly understood what had to be done for optimum results and our allotment site was the poorer when he found that longer factory shift hours prevented his continuing the happy and rewarding time he had spent on his plot.

It is a sheer waste of seeds, time and labour to try to grow brussels sprouts if your soil is not highly fertile. The plants will grow after a fashion but you will not pick one decent sprout from the lot of them. The ground must drain well and the site should be quite open. It is generally easier to get better sprouts on an allotment than from a small- to medium-size garden. Gardens lack the open, airy aspects. There are very many varieties of sprouts around. A good way of finding out which one is best suited to your area is to ask any local gardener who grows really good sprouts which variety he grows. Varieties which have delighted me include Peer Gynt, Prince Askold and Roodnerf-Vremo Inter. These produce sprouts when I want them – December and January. The sprouts are also of medium size. Sow seeds in April and move the plants on to a nursery bed. When selecting plants at planting time in June, reject any which have bent stems. Reject, too, the occasional 'blind' plant – this lacks a central growing point. Inspect the roots of any bought plants for Club Root swellings (see p. 46).

In the rotation of crops brussels sprouts are often grown where potatoes were grown in the previous summer. When possible, spread garden compost over the firmed bed at planting time. See pp. 41–8 for information on planting, pests and diseases. Keep down weeds, and as soon as the plants are fully-grown discontinue hoeing. Not only would you damage the foliage but you would also almost certainly damage the near-surface roots of the brussels during hoeing. Cabbage caterpillars are rarely much of a nuisance on sprouts plants. Pick off the few you see. If for some special reason you want earlier-than-usual sprouts pinch out the central growing point of plants in early September. As winter approaches, remove any dying, yellow leaves and add to the compost pile. If you garden in a very windy area you may find other gardeners tie their brussels plants to strong bamboo canes. Do this, too, if you consider it necessary.

If all has gone well, start harvesting sprouts from the bottom of the plants and work upwards at each picking. During late January you will be picking the tiny sprouts near the top and in February you can cut off the tops of the plants for use as 'greens'. If you nipped out the growing points in September there will be no brussels tops worth cutting. Things have not gone wrong if the sprouts right at the base of the plants are not as well formed as the rest. They have gone wrong if almost all of the sprouts are open ('blown' in gardener's jargon). The reasons for this happening are many. Perhaps your soil was too loose at planting time. Perhaps the former plot-holder had used nitrogenous manures or fertilizer on the grand scale and residues remain in the soil. Perhaps the plants were short of moisture when needed in high summer and when the plants have to make quick growth.

Cabbage

Falls into four main groups – summer, autumn, winter, spring. There is also red cabbage. The savoy cabbage has very puckered leaves and is included here under the section devoted to winter cabbages. In general cabbages are sown, planted and cultivated in the manner outlined under the heading *Brassicas*.

Summer cabbage

Although gardeners with heated greenhouses frequently sow cabbage seeds in boxes during February, their hopes of very early summer cabbages are dashed when they find themselves with dozens of weak seedlings in the greenhouse and snow or bitter winds outside. If you have an unheated greenhouse or a cold frame you may safely sow cabbage in early March knowing that by the time the seedlings will have to be set out in the garden or allotment, weather conditions ought to be favourable. If they are not, you will have to give the young plants cloche protection for about a fortnight. For my own earliest summer cabbages I wait until late March or the first week of April before sowing seeds of Greyhound or Golden Acre (Primo) in the greenhouse border. The plants are put out in the garden a month or so later. More summer cabbage is sown along with other brassicas in mid April. The seedlings grow so quickly that it hardly seems worth while moving them from the seed to the nursery bed. Because of my work in evaluating vegetable varieties I ring the changes quite a bit and I can also recommend June Star, Emerald Cross, Vienna (Babyhead) and Wiam. Unless the family is extremely fond of cabbages in summer there is no reason to grow more than a couple of dozen. Most of us prefer to eat and enjoy a wide range of summer vegetables. Was it a French gardener who said 'The English have three vegetables; two of them are cabbage'?

Autumn cabbage

When the last dwarf french or runner beans are picked in late September or in October, the gardener and his family fall back once again on cabbages as a second vegetable. Autumn Monarch and Autumn Pride are useful for cutting in October and November. Unfortunately these cabbages tend to split if the autumn is a wet one. You may prefer to plant out a few extra seedlings of the summer cabbage Wiam instead. This small, very compact cabbage stands without splitting well into autumn. If you go in for the real and larger autumn cabbages, sow seeds along with other brassicas (see pp. 41–2) in April, transplant seedlings to a nursery bed in May and plant out in June or early July.

Winter cabbage

January King is the standard winter cabbage and it's a good one at that. Sow seeds in the brassica seed bed in April, move on to a nursery bed in May and set out plants in June or early July. Start cutting well-hearted, tight cabbages in November and cut as and when you wish until after Christmas. A savoy cabbage like Ice Queen is also a good choice for winter cabbage apart from the fact that the very puckered leaves provide first-class camouflage for brassica-eating caterpillars. The camouflage makes it quite difficult to find the caterpillars, which stick out like sore thumbs on brassicas with smoother foliage. Whether one should leave stumps of winter cabbages in the ground after the cabbages have been harvested or whether the stumps should be dug up immediately and consigned to the compost heap is a debatable point. Those who fear that aphids on old stumps may move to tender, young plants of spring cabbage, carry out the latter procedure. Other gardeners, and I am one of them, permit the stumps to produce young shoots for use in the kitchen as 'spring greens' before the stumps are dug up. When pulling up stumps of cabbages and other brassicas check for signs of Club Root (see p. 46). Cut off and burn infected roots; add the stems to the compost pile.

Red cabbage

Niggerhead is typical of this sort of cabbage which, in Britain at any rate, is usually grown solely for pickling. This is a pity because red cabbage is excellent cooked with apple and onion and served with pork. That is how most Europeans like their red cabbage, and so do I. Sow and grow red cabbage as autumn/winter cabbages. Harvest cabbages as and when you wish between late October and Christmas.

Spring cabbage

Cabbages for cutting between late April and late June are termed 'spring cabbages'. There are two very important points connected with them. First, do not sow until late July if you live in the north of England or in Scotland. Midland and southern gardeners should wait till early August. This is about the right time, too, for sowing in most parts of Ireland and Wales. Secondly, make sure you choose a variety recommended for spring use. My own preferences are April and Harbinger. Both are compact, tight, cone-shaped, good-flavoured cabbages. If local gardeners tell you that Offenham-Flower of Spring is the variety to choose, by all means give it a try. I find it slow to heart up. In the north, Durham Early and Durham Elf are liked. These do well in southern England, as I saw when I grew them. See pp. 41–2 for sowing details. Pay special care to watering if the summer is a dry one. Do not move the seedlings to a nursery bed and have ground dug ready for planting out some time in September. Usually the spring cabbage bed is sited on a plot from which first or second early potatoes have been dug. When forking over the ground, make sure that all potato tubers, however tiny, are removed. If they are not, potato plants pop up like garden weeds among the spring cabbages during April. It is usually considered as a waste of good freezer space to blanch and freeze one's surplus garden-grown cabbage. However, spring cabbages are so tasty that I always freeze the last few.

Capsicum (sweet pepper)

Do not grow these unless you are sure that the family eats them with relish. You can check on this by buying a few. If they are liked, then grow some four or six plants in your greenhouse. Canapé is a popular variety. Sow seeds and treat the seedlings as if they are tomatoes (see p. 108ff.) The plants grow to a height of around 75 cm (2½ ft) and are bushy. It is rather a waste of good greenhouse space to have capsicum plants in the greenhouse border. Fortunately capsicums do well in pots. I sow two or three seeds in 9-cm (3½-in) peat Jiffies filled with Levington Potting Compost in late April or early May in the greenhouse. I reduce the seedlings to leave one only in each pot. By late May the young plants need potting on into 22-cm (9-in) diameter pots. I use ordinary top soil from the garden in these pots. During July the tomato plants in the greenhouse borders begin to shade the shorter capsicum plants so I move them out into the garden. If the summer is a hot one the pot capsicums are stood in a sunny position; in cooler summers I sink two pots in the ground quite close to each other and then erect a couple of Expandite Low Barn cloches around them. Stand the cloches on end and to prevent them being blown over support them with strong bamboo canes. Pot capsicum plants need watering well and often. There are no cultivation problems. You can pick your peppers when green in August or leave a few to change to bright red in September.

Carrot

Carrots are rather choosey about soil conditions. Ideally you need a sandy loam which never dries out during periods of summer drought. The soil must not be too stony nor must it contain 'pockets' of manure or incompletely decomposed garden compost. It is up to us gardeners to get our garden soils into as suitable a condition as possible for carrots to thrive. Hints on how to deal with your garden soil for the production of vegetables generally (see Chapter 2) will, if followed, lead to your own garden or allotment soil becoming ideal for carrot production.

Carrots must never be permitted to be short of water, otherwise they will split when heavy rain falls. However good your soil conditions may be, do not be too disappointed if the carrot crop is bad if the summer is a dry one and the allotment site lacks a water supply. There are many good varieties of carrot. My own favourite, Autumn King, is a fairly long carrot noted for its good keeping quality in store. If you are aiming at early carrots and are sowing in a cold frame or beneath cloches (see Chapter 2) then sow the handsome, shorter Nantes-Tip Top. One of the troubles with carrot growing is weed competition when the carrot seedlings are tiny. If you sow seeds in the open garden and when the soil is not all that warm, you have quite a wait for the carrot seeds to germinate and the seedlings to show above ground. In the meantime our native wild plants germinate in and around the rows and many a new gardener wonders whether it may be better to dig the lot in and start all over again. Early spring sowings are also so often plagued with Carrot Fly (see p. 56). I wait until mid to late May before sowing carrot seeds in 2·5-cm (1-in) deep seed drills spaced 30 cm (1 ft) apart. If the ground is dry I flood the drills with water before sprinkling the seeds evenly in them. If you know that you are too heavy-handed when you sow carrots, mix the seeds with a trowel-full of dry earth or sand and sow the mixture. After sowing the seeds cover with soil, using a rake or your boots, label the rows and wait for seedlings to appear within a fortnight. As soon as you can see rows of seedlings, use a Dutch hoe to rid spaces between the rows of weed seedlings. When hoeing around carrots take all possible care that the hoe does not nick the seedlings. Not only will the carrot be damaged but the odour from the wound may advertise the presence of your carrots to local lady Carrot Flies.

Carrot seedlings have to be thinned unless you sow pelleted seeds spaced at about 2·5 cm (1 in) apart. Always thin when the soil is very wet so that the thinnings can be pulled quite easily out of the ground. Start just as soon as some are large enough for use in the kitchen. Spread the work over a fortnight so that finally all carrots left to grow on have sufficient space for continued good growth. Leave 2·5 cm (1 in) around each carrot plant: this is adequate. Try not to break carrot foliage when thinning and hurry too-small-to-use thinnings and the foliage of young carrots for eating to the compost heap. Bury within the heap to prevent Carrot Fly troubles. Do not leave carrots in the ground after October. If you do, slugs will attack them; the carrots will also lose flavour. I dig my carrots on a dry day during the first week of October. Carrots can be stored sandwich-fashion between moist sand or peat in a hole in the ground in the garden or in a green-house. They may be stored in this way in boxes or bins in an outhouse, a cellar or garden shed. When preparing the roots for storage, rub off any soil adhering to them and cut back the foliage to about 1·25 cm ($\frac{1}{2}$ in) above the carrots. Or they can be frozen for use in stews, soups and casseroles.

Carrot Fly is an accepted hazard in carrot growing. Because female Carrot Flies are guided to this vegetable by the odour of the foliage, damage is far more likely to occur to allotment-grown carrots than to those grown in a garden. This is because on an allotment site every plot-holder goes in for carrots, so the smell of carrots is more pronounced than it is in the average garden. It has already been suggested that every care should be taken when weeding or thinning carrots to diminish the aroma emitted by carrot foliage. The female flies lay eggs just below the soil surface and alongside carrot seedlings in May. The larvae hatch within about a week and bore into the tiny carrots, riddling them with holes. You can detect an attack by the change in colour of carrot foliage, which turns to a rusty brown or has a reddish appearance. Plants may wilt and die. A fellow plot-holder tells me that he escapes Carrot Fly damage because he grows carrots alongside onions. He says the mixed aromas of carrot and onion deter both the Carrot Fly and the Onion Fly. The idea seems worth trying.

Cauliflower

Because this vegetable must have rich soil and adequate water coupled with first-class drainage, most gardeners try growing cauliflowers once or twice and then give up. By all means try cauliflower growing but if you are aiming at choice, snowy heads between August and November and things go wrong, you will appreciate just how difficult cauliflower growing can be. To have late summer and autumn cauliflowers, sow seed of All the Year Round or Autumn Giant along with other brassicas in April (see pp. 41ff.), move the seedlings to a nursery bed in May, if you so wish, and set out the plants where they are to grow in June. Keep well watered in dry weather, hoe occasionally to prevent weeds, inspect occasionally for caterpillars, picking off any you come across and, if all goes well, cut snowy white cauliflowers in due course. If several cauliflowers form heads at the same time you may harvest them all and freeze them if you have a freezer. Alternatively, break a large leaf over the heads when they are forming. The shaded heads will not turn yellow as quickly as they often do in bright weather. Always harvest cauliflowers when they are white and firm; yellowish, older cauliflowers are suitable only for pickling, I think.

Just as late summer/autumn cauliflowers can be difficult to grow, spring-heading cauliflowers are easy. Here again it is important to choose the correct variety. I find English Wonder-Reading Giant excellent. Seeds are sown along with other brassicas in the special seed bed (see p. 42) during April. The seedlings are moved to a nursery bed a month later and plants are set out during June or early July. Apart from any necessary weeding and watering there is nothing else to do but await with pleasurable anticipation the formation of the cauliflowers in April. Yes, from seed sowing to cutting the cauliflowers takes an entire year but they are worth waiting for. In frosty or very sunny weather I break a large leaf over the cauliflowers to prevent frost damage or yellowing of the curds.

Celeriac

This is a form of celery grown, not for succulent stems, but for its large turnip-like root. Because the plants need a long growing season it is advisable to sow seeds in a heated greenhouse in mid March. A temperature of 65°F (18°C) leads to good, even germination. Seeds may be sown broadcast (sprinkled unevenly) in a seed tray and the seedlings transferred to small pots. Because my greenhouse is not heated I wait until the latter half of April before sowing, but I am sure my celeriac would be larger were I

to sow earlier and in heat. However, here is my own method of
celeriac propagation.

Three or four seeds are sown in 9-cm (3½-in) peat pots filled with
Levington Potting Compost. The compost is kept moist but not
over-wet and when the seedlings are about 2·5 cm (1 in) tall, I
thin them to leave a strong one in each pot. After hardening off
the plants in late May or early June I tear away any dry parts of
the peat pots and set out the plants in the garden at 30 cm (1 ft)
apart, leaving 45 cm (15 ins) between rows. To harden off greenhouse-grown plants, I put the pots in seed trays or Dutch trays
and stand them out in the garden for a few days. The plants are
returned to the greenhouse each evening except on the evening
before I anticipate planting. They spend that night in the garden.

For celeriac the ground must be very fertile; spread a thick
mulch of garden compost over the sunny site where celeriac is to
grow. When setting out celeriac, do not plant deeply. Throughout
its growth the swelling root must sit on the soil. When hoeing
around the plants, draw soil away from them. Tear off any leafy
growths which sometimes appear near the base of the plants. The
celeries are marsh plants so ensure that celeriac always has plenty
of moisture at the roots. Pull celeriac for use as and when you
wish as soon as they are large enough; this is really a winter
vegetable and a substitute for celery. Celeriac may be left in the
garden in milder parts of the country until November at least. I
consider it better to harvest the entire crop during October and to
store the roots in a cool, dry shed or a similar spot. Store as
carrots (see p. 56). When preparing celeriac for storing trim back
the roots and cut off all of the leaves apart from the small tuft at
the top of each celeriac. Any leaves in good condition may be
frozen for use in winter soups. Washed, peeled and grated celeriac
may be added to salads. Wash, peel and slice thickly before
cooking celeriac.

Celery

As with celeriac, results are likely to be better if seeds are sown
under glass in March and at a temperature of about 65°F (18°C).
Sow and harden off plants in the manner suggested for celeriac.
Here again you are dealing with a hungry, thirsty vegetable so the

soil must be highly fertile and you must be prepared to water well and often in dry summer weather. Easiest celery to grow is American Green. This is fairly new to Britain and is not as well known as it deserves to be. All you have to do is to raise your plants and set them out in the garden 22 cm (9 ins) apart in early June. Leave 30 cm (1 ft) between rows. Do not plant deeply. Use a Dutch hoe to prevent weeds and tear off any side growths at the bases of the plants during July and August. You can start cutting the heads (complete plants) for use in early September or leave them to grow larger. But bear in mind that American Green is not frost-hardy and unless frozen does not store. (*Note:* frozen celery is of use only in cooked dishes.) So the crop must be harvested and eaten before really cold winter weather sets in.

Self-blanching celery is equally easy to grow and Golden Self Blanching is a good variety (for blanching see p. 60). This type of celery is not as self-blanching as the name suggests and should be grown in garden frames. Raise your plants and set them out during late May or early June. Space plants at 22 cm (9 ins) apart. Flood the bed with water after planting and keep the frame light closed for a few days. Then, prop up the frame light by about 5 cm (2 ins) during the day but close it at night. Remove the frame light altogether in mid or late June. Keep the plants very moist and remove weeds. When the plants are growing well, spread dry straw to a depth of about 22 cm (9 ins) around the plants. The straw may attract slugs, in which case place slug bait beneath the straw. Tear off any side growths produced around the bases of the plants. This celery is ready for use in August and September. It is not frost-hardy.

Celery for use in autumn and winter has to be blanched. There are many varieties from which to choose and I suggest Giant White-Solid White, Giant Red and Giant Pink. Raise your plants and harden them off for planting in a 30-cm (1 ft) deep, 45-cm (15-in) wide trench during June. Unless given adequate nourishment your trench celery will be a wash-out. It pays to re-place the soil at the bottom of the trench with a mixture of well-rotted farmyard or horse manure, garden compost and lawn mowings. Drench this mixture with water. When the water has drained in, firm the bottom of the trench and plant two rows of celery with plants at 22 cm (9 ins) apart. When digging the trench stack the excavated soil neatly alongside it. You will not need this soil until August so you may set out lettuce seedlings on it or sow radish. Cultivation until August consists of removing any weeds and keeping the bottom of the trench really wet.

Blanching is carried out in three stages. Make a start in mid August. Hold each plant tightly to prevent soil entering the heart and heap about 10 cm (4 ins) of crumbly soil around the plants. Water well and a fortnight later, take more of the soil stacked alongside the row to earth up the plants again. Two or three weeks later, tie the foliage of each plant together fairly loosely and use more crumbly soil to earth up finally to just below the green leaves. Firm the banked up soil around the plants with a spade. Spread a little straw over the plants in November as a protection against frost and snow. Start digging your trench celery in November and dig as and when wanted until February.

Slugs can make a mess of trench celery if the garden or allotment harbours these pests in excess of the smaller numbers to be expected in all gardens. If the slugs take up residence within the heart of this form of celery there is nothing you can do about it apart from digging up the whole lot and freezing all undamaged sticks before the slugs do more damage. Celery fly maggots are a nuisance on all forms of celery in some seasons. The maggots tunnel into the foliage; affected leaves have transparent patches. Search for the maggots and squeeze them inside their burrows in the foliage.

Celery is not a vegetable I would recommend for plot-holders in drier parts of the country or where the allotment site is at some distance from the home because of the regular and copious amounts of water which this thirsty subject has to have through the summer.

Chicory

In recent years chicory chicons have become well known because many greengrocers have them for sale in winter. Few gardeners, however, grow this vegetable. The reason? Probably that most gardeners consider this and any other less usually grown vegetable as something rather difficult. I hope that what I write here will assure you that chicory growing is quite easy. You need seeds. Witloof is the variety to sow and wait until early June in the north (mid June in the south) before sowing the seeds fairly thinly in a 2·5-cm (1-in) deep seed drill. If you are sowing more than a single row, leave 30 cm (1 ft) between rows. Flood the seed drills with water if the soil is dry and sow when this has drained away. When seedlings are about 5 cm (2 ins) tall, thin them out to leave strong young plants at 22 cm (9 ins) apart. No further cultivation is necessary apart from putting a Dutch hoe between the rows as and when any weeds appear. Water in very droughty summer weather. In November dig up all of the parsnip-like roots. Discard any which are thin or fanged and stand those you are retaining in a shallow trench. Pack soil around the roots to fill the trench. Chicons are new growths produced by the roots. The chicons are blanched so that they are not bitter in taste. I force chicory roots for supplies of blanched chicons in my greenhouse and this method could be followed in a garden frame if you have no greenhouse. Rake a part of the greenhouse border level and then, using a cabbage dibber, make holes quite closely together. Fill the holes with water and leave it to drain into the soil. Take several chicory roots from the trench, cut back the foliage to leave no more than 2·5 cm (1 in) of root. Also trim back the roots by the same amount if they are extra long. The prepared roots are then planted in the dibber holes, and the bed is covered with a 2·5-cm (1-in) thick layer of dry straw. Dry soil is then shovelled on to the straw so that this is weighed down. In my greenhouse chicons are not ready for cutting for about two months; in a heated greenhouse they will be ready earlier. You will see the noses of the chicons pushing through the straw and soil cover. Move the soil and straw so that you can cut the chicons from the roots. I have forced chicons in boxes and larger flowerpots indoors. If you try this, fill the boxes or pots with moist soil from the garden and make sure that the containers are well covered so that no light reaches the chicons. Light leads to yellowish chicons which are bitter. Always use chicory chicons immediately after cutting. If left about chicons toughen and tend to lose their fine white colour. Chicory may be blanched for freezer storage and for use later on in cooked dishes. Fresh chicory may be cooked or served in salads.

Chinese cabbage

This is generally considered as one of the most difficult vegetables to grow well in Britain. If seeds are sown earlier than about mid June, or are not well watered in dry weather, the seedlings 'bolt' (throw up flowering stems). Sow between mid June to mid July in 2·5-cm (1-in) deep seed drills spaced at 30 cm (1 ft). Thin out seedlings to leave young plants at 30 cm (1 ft) apart when they are quite tiny and when the ground is moist or you will loosen the roots of the seedlings you are going to leave to grow. Hoe very occasionally to prevent weeds and do remember to keep the plants well-watered. When plants have made plenty of spreading leaves tie the foliage of each plant loosely as with Cos lettuces (see p. 78). In 1975 Suttons Seeds introduced a new F_1 hybrid Chinese cabbage, 'Sampan'. This is by far the best variety I have grown and I strongly recommend it. Chinese cabbage should be cut for use as soon as the heads (the entire cabbage) are large and fairly tight. The cabbages wilt rapidly after harvesting and do not store well. Any surplus to immediate requirements may be blanched and frozen for use as a cooked vegetable in winter. Freshly cut Chinese cabbage may be cooked as ordinary cabbage or used in salads to replace lettuce.

Chinese mustard

Pac-Choy is the variety usually mentioned in books and in the horticultural press. A year or so ago Thompson & Morgan of Ipswich sent me seeds of their mustard 'Tendergreen'. In my view, this newer variety is far superior to Pac-Choy. Sow and cultivate as Chinese cabbage. You may leave the plants loose or tie them as for Cos lettuce (see p. 78). Pick leaves from loose plants as for picking spinach (see p. 105); cut tied-in heads when they are well formed and fairly tight. Use this vegetable fresh in salads or cooked. Any surplus may be blanched and frozen.

Chives (see herbs, p. 70)

Corn salad

Also known as Lamb's Lettuce and a British weed. The cultivated form comes from Europe and has more succulent leaves. It may be sown at almost any time during the growing season but sow in August and September for a supply of Corn salad to use as a lettuce substitute in late winter and spring. Sow in 2·5-cm (1-in) deep seed drills spaced 20 cm (8 ins) apart. If the ground is dry, flood the drills with water and sow seeds fairly evenly when it has drained away. Cover the seeds with the excavated soil and use a rake to leave things looking neat. Thin the seedlings to 15 cm (6 ins) apart and use an onion hoe and your fingers to prevent annual weeds like chickweed from smothering them. Corn salad is a low-growing, straggly plant from which one may break off portions of the foliage. Alternatively, pull up complete plants. Always wash the foliage well to rid it of gritty dirt.

Courgettes (See Vegetable marrow, p. 124)

Cress (American Cress)

This is not the cress of Mustard and Cress nor is it American. Another name for it is Land Cress. It is of European origin and is sometimes found naturalized on waste ground in Britain. Like Corn salad, American Cress is a low growing plant and a lettuce substitute. Like Corn salad, too, it is of greater value when there are unlikely to be lettuces in the garden. It is therefore usual to delay sowing until mid August. Unlike most vegetables, American Cress likes some shade and a north-facing border is very suitable. Sow in 2·5-cm (1-in) deep seed drills spaced at 30 cm (1 ft) apart. If the soil is dry flood the drills before sowing seeds fairly thinly. Thin seedlings to 20 cm (8 ins) apart and hoe occasionally to control weeds. For winter supplies cover the plants with cloches in late October. Alternatively, dig up the plants and replant them in a garden frame. Pick leaves and shoots as and when wanted in salads or sandwiches. The flavour is very similar to watercress but slightly hotter. (See also Mustard and Cress, p. 80.)

Cucumbers

Cucumber varieties can be divided rather arbitrarily into two sorts – non-hardy and fairly hardy. Most of the cucumbers seen in our shops are grown in greenhouses. Although newer varieties continue to be introduced, you cannot go far wrong if you stick to older sorts like Telegraph Improved and Conqueror. If your green-house is heated by all means make an early start by sowing seeds in March at a temperature of 21°C (70°F), but you must be pre-pared to keep the seedlings at around 18°C (65°F) minimum. Cucumber seeds need heat to germinate and if subjected to low temperatures either die or produce disappointing crops. One other point with cucumber growing: because cucumber plants like a steamy, Turkish bath sort of atmosphere, it is unwise to try growing cucumbers and tomatoes in the same greenhouse. The tomato plant cannot bear an over-wet environment. True, many gardeners do grow cucumbers and tomatoes together and get good crops of both but things can go wrong. If you live in warmer parts, wait until late April or the first week of May before sowing cucumber seeds in an unheated greenhouse and rely on trapped sun heat to effect good germination and to keep seedlings growing steadily. In other parts of the country you can reduce greenhouse fuel bills by sowing during the last half of April and by providing sufficient heat to keep greenhouse temperatures at around 21°C (70°F) until the seeds germinate and then permitting temperatures to fall to 18°C (65°F). You will be able to rely on sun heat to have 18°C (65°F) as a minimum day temperature and some heat will be necessary at night until late June to retain a night temperature of from 16–18°C (60–65°F). Sow two seeds at a depth of about 1·25 cm ($\frac{1}{2}$ in) in each 9-cm ($3\frac{1}{2}$-in) size flowerpot. I much prefer peat Jiffy pots because the roots of seedlings can pass through the base of the pot instead of curling round like a clock spring, as they often do in other sorts of pot. Also, with Jiffies you plant the pot, so that the roots of young plants are not disturbed. This is an important point in the growing of cucumbers (and melons and vegetable marrows).

When the first true leaf (this is the real, roughish sort of cu-cumber leaf, unlike the smooth, elliptic shape of the two seed leaves) has begun to grow, pinch off at soil level the second weaker seedling in each pot. If you tug out this unwanted seedling you may damage or loosen the roots of the seedling you wish to retain. Keep the compost in the pots moist and stand the pots apart so that each seedling has room for good growth. The plants can be set out at 60 cm (2 ft) apart in the greenhouse border when they have made about four *true* leaves. Cucumbers are greedy, thirsty plants so the greenhouse border must have been well enriched with rotted horse manure or garden compost. To provide sufficient plant foods for good growth and good cropping, I spread a 2·5-cm (1-in) thick mulch of garden compost over the entire greenhouse border. Cucumber plants are subject to rotting at the base of the main stem if water lodges around the plant. To prevent this I plant so that 1·25 cm ($\frac{1}{2}$ in) or so of the soil ball (the compost in the pot) is above the level of the soil of the bed. I rig up a framework of bamboo canes linked with horizontal wires to which the growing plants are tied loosely. Plants are kept moist at the roots and when the plants reach the top of the supports (about 1·8 m or 6 ft), I nip off the growing point at the top of each plant. If any female flowers are produced on the main stems of the plants they, too, are pinched off. You can recognize female flowers easily; they have a tiny cucumber behind them. My aim is to get the plants to make good growth and produce lots of cucumbers on lateral (side) shoots. When small cucumbers on the laterals are just swelling I pinch off the tip of the laterals at two leaves beyond a swelling cucumber. Greenhouse cucumbers like Telegraph and Conqueror also have male flowers. These should be pinched off at the bud stage so that female flowers are not pollinated by male pollen. Pollinated greenhouse cucumbers can become bulbous in shape; it is also believed that they can become bitter but I feel that bitterness in cucumbers is due to low temperatures causing the cucumbers to swell slowly. Always cut cucumbers when they appear to be of the right size to you and do not aim to have super-sized cucumbers as these lack flavour. Cutting often encourages more cucumber flowers to set fruits.

Improved Telegraph and Conqueror may also be grown in an unheated garden frame in southern England. Bear in mind that the frame must be large; in a frame measuring at least 1·8 m (6 ft) long and 75 cm (2½ ft) wide one cucumber plant may be permitted to ramble from one end of the frame to the other. Nip off the growing point of the cucumber plant a few days after planting so that the plant makes two or more side shoots. Train these to the corners of the frame and stop these laterals when they reach the corners (by nipping out the growing point of the shoot). Keep the plants well watered in sunny weather, pinch off male flowers if you can find them among the mass of foliage and any female flowers on the main single stem or on any of the main laterals. If the soil is not as good as it should be you can apply liquid feeds when cucumbers are swelling. Liquid feeds may be made by soaking a sack of horse, cow, sheep or other animal dung in a tub of water. Do not apply the feed neat; dilute it so that it is the colour of weak tea. Alternatively, feed with a general (liquid) fertilizer recommended for vegetables and dilute to the manufacturer's instructions. If the glass of a garden frame or greenhouse is new, bright summer sunlight may scorch the plants. In very bright summer weather apply a little shade (such as whitewash) to the exterior of the glass. Green polythene shading can be fixed to the interior greenhouse roof. Always rid the glass of shading when days become overcast. In very hot weather the plants will benefit from being sprayed with clean cold water of an afternoon. If you go in for growing the newer all-female flowering cucumbers in the greenhouse, note any special instructions the seedsmen may suggest as regards the prevention of over-cropping.

Among varieties of fairly hardy cucumbers the newer sorts should be chosen for growing outdoors in warmer parts of the country. Varieties like Burpless Green King, Burpless Tasty Green and Burpless Early are long and tasty. Greenhouse heating costs could be cut drastically if these were chosen for greenhouse cultivation in colder parts of Britain. How well these or other fairly hardy cucumbers will do outdoors in the north depends on the summer weather. A cold frame or a few cloches could well help if you are a northern gardener and have no greenhouse yet wish to have your own cucumbers for summer salads. These garden aids are also of great use in ensuring that cucumber seeds germinate well and that seedlings are not shocked by a cold spell in June.

The southern gardener may simply sow seeds at 1·25 cm (½ in) deep and where the plants are to grow. Wait until mid May before doing this and sow groups of two or three seeds at 45 cm (18 ins) apart – but think ahead. The plants will roam over the ground and each will need about a square metre (yard) of surface area. You can hasten germination by setting a jam jar (open end downwards) over each station (spot where seeds are sown). Take jars away when the seedlings need more space. Pinch off surplus seedlings when small, to leave one at each station. Hardier cucumbers are often referred to as 'ridge cucumbers'.

Cucumbers do not like having their feet in water. If, therefore, your garden soil does not drain well it will pay you to grow these cucumbers on a slightly raised bed. This could be a metre (yard) wide and 20 cm (8 ins) above the surrounding soil. The bed may be kept in position by wooden boards or be simply a raised, oval hump. To give my own open garden cucumbers an early start I sow in peat pots in late April or early May. The pots are housed in the greenhouse or in a garden frame. Before moving the plants to where they are to grow I harden them off (see p. 58) in early June. Garden compost is spread liberally over the bed and when planting I ensure that the top of the soil ball is at just above the level of the surrounding soil so that no stem rot may take place. When the plants have seven *true* leaves, I pinch off the growing point of each plant. No more pruning is carried out. Cucumbers on plants left to trail over the ground are seldom as straight as those produced on plants growing upwards in a greenhouse. To have straight, long cucumbers on outdoor-grown plants, provide them with a trellis. This should be from 1·2–1·8 m (4–6 ft) high and may be metal or plastic garden mesh or simply a few stout, tall poles with several horizontal wires. Plants should be set out (or seeds sown) at 30 cm (1 ft) apart alongside the trellis. Tie the plants loosely to the trellis and pinch off the growing points of plants when they reach the top. No other pruning is necessary. I have had excellent results with Kaga, Kyoto and Baton Vert grown as trellis-trained plants and have no doubt that the Burpless range of cucumbers would succeed equally well. For gherkins to pickle choose Venlo Pickling and grow the plants as trailers over the ground.

Apart from slug damage to seedlings, cucumber growing is

seldom beset by pest and disease problems. Because ripe pollen from male flowers has to reach the female flowers – a job bees and other insects carry out – hardier cucumbers are unlikely to crop well in garden frames or under cloches unless the gardener makes sure that flying insects can gain easy entrance and exit to and from the plants when they are flowering in July, August and September. Never remove male flowers on plants of hardier cucumbers as is the practice in the cultivation of the less hardy greenhouse sorts.

Egg plant (See Aubergine, p. 35)

Endive

There are two forms – the Batavian and the Curled. The curled sort is preferred by those who know this vegetable and this is the endive sold in shops. I grow 'Green Curled' as a lettuce substitute for late autumn and early winter use. Sow fairly thickly in 2·5-cm (1-in) deep seed drills in mid June with rows 37 cm (15 ins) apart. Fill the drills with water before sowing if the ground is dry. Thin seedlings to 30 cm (12 ins) apart, keep free from weeds and water in dry weather. By late September you will have handsome, dark green lettuce-like plants but with foliage which is far too bitter to eat.

Shop endive is usually partially blanched; to do this, tie each plant fairly loosely together when they are dry as with Cos lettuce. A few weeks later untie a plant for use. The heart should be yellow. Partially blanched endive (the yellow and green foliage) should be chopped finely and mixed with other salad ingredients. Fully blanched endive has a superb flavour resembling that of chicory. Dig up the plants and replant them with the foliage loosely tied and set a large pot over each one so that all light is excluded. Do the job on a dry day and when any dew has dried off. Three weeks later take off the pot. You should have creamy-white endive. Fully blanched or partially blanched endive should be eaten within an hour or so of harvesting when it is at its tastiest.

Fennel (Florence Fennel)

This vegetable is also known as Finocchio and is a close relative of Sweet Fennel, a tall-growing British wild plant. The foliage of Florence Fennel lacks the highly aromatic, aniseed aroma of Sweet Fennel. The edible part of this rarely grown luxury vegetable is the swollen base of the stem. Sow seeds in April, May or June in 2·5-cm (1-in) deep seed drills spaced at 30 cm (1 ft) apart. Thin seedlings to leave sturdy young plants at 22 cm (9 ins) apart in the row. Hoe occasionally to prevent weed growth and water in dry spells. Harvest for use when the stem bases are fully swollen. If you are not sure whether you like this vegetable, buy a couple of stem bases from a specialist greengrocer and try them first, otherwise you will waste time and garden space growing something you may not enjoy. Fennel may not be a great success in colder parts of Britain unless the summer weather is really good.

Garlic (see Herbs, p. 71)

Gherkin (see Cucumbers, p. 64)

Herbs

Herbs differ from vegetables in that, while we grow vegetables to eat, we grow herbs to flavour our food. The more commonly known herbs to be found in the kitchen garden need similar growing conditions to vegetables. If you only have a patio, a paved backyard or town balcony, herb growing is ideal. Most herbs do well in window-boxes, tubs or 25-cm (10-in) clay or plastic pots. Old plastic wash bowls and buckets (with holes made in the base to permit free drainage) are also excellent growing containers for most herbs. You can always bring home some good top soil in the boot of the car when visiting a country cousin or buy a bag of Levington Potting Compost. Young herb plants are often offered for sale in garden shops, garden centres and chain stores. At planting time, remove the plants from clay, plastic, polythene or card pots, trying not to disturb the rooting system.

Bay

Buy a young tree. A 60-cm (2-ft) high tree may spend two years in a 22-cm (9-in) diameter pot. Then pot on into a 30-cm (12-in) container. (Bay trees often stand at the entrance to restaurants in larger cities.) Trees may be shaped by judicious clipping. Leaves are picked as they are wanted; strip leaves from clippings to be dried and stored.

Chives

May be raised from seed but more usually the gardener starts with offsets (pieces taken from the roots of clumps of plants).

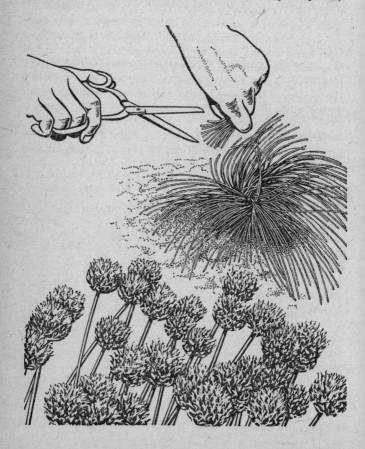

Plant offsets 15 cm (6 ins) apart in spring or autumn. Chives make good edging plants round the kitchen or flower garden. It takes about a year for plants to become established. Cut foliage close to the soil in spring when you wish to use it. More tender foliage will be produced after the first cut. If you want to have a flower display of deep mauve blooms, leave a few clumps especially for this purpose; chives bloom in May. Dig up established clumps every fourth autumn, split the clumps into small sections and replant these elsewhere in the garden or in fresh soil or compost in plant containers.

Garlic

May be raised from seeds but is usually propagated from cloves – sections taken from garlic bulbs. Plant these at 2·5 cm (1 in) deep and 15 cm (6 in) apart during March. Dig the crop in late July or August when the green foliage has started to yellow. Hang in small bunches in full sun to dry off before you rub off the dry roots and foliage. Store in a dry, cool place. Put aside one or two bulbs from which cloves may be taken for planting next spring.

Horseradish

This herb is propagated by planting pieces of root taken from established clumps. You may buy suitable planting pieces or (providing you can recognize the plant) dig up a clump growing on waste land. Dig only when the leaves have died down in autumn and choose pieces of thick root – each with a triangular tight bud cluster at the top – for replanting at 60 cm (2 ft) apart. This is not a herb for container growing unless you have a deep tub or plastic dustbin. Leave the plants to get established and wait for two seasons before digging roots for use. The dug roots may be stored in boxes of moist sand, peat or soil in a cool place. When digging horseradish in autumn always make sure that every part of the root system is got out, otherwise it will become a great nuisance in your garden. Choose pieces of root for replanting elsewhere in the garden or allotment (see next page).

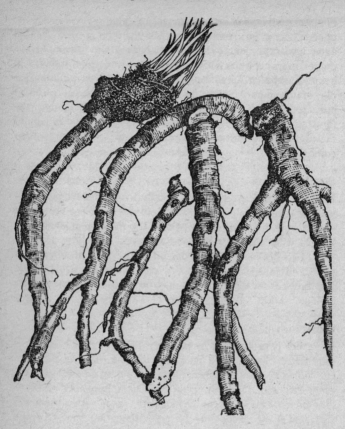

Mint

There are many mints. If you already have mint growing in your garden and its flavour suits you and the family, then continue growing it. If you have no mint and wish to know what sort to grow, I suggest Spearmint. Plant at 7·5 cm (3 ins) apart in a special mint bed. This herb is invasive and must be kept under strict control to prevent it from making a take-over bid for the entire garden. It is the roots of mint which spread rapidly. They run along the surface of the soil and just below soil level. A strip of metal lawn edging embedded in the ground and encircling the mint patch can keep mint in bounds. When the patch looks very overcrowded, dig up the entire bed in late autumn or early winter, untangle the mass of roots and replant them in a new bed. Just lay 15–22 cm (6–9 ins) lengths of mint root in very shallow trenches spaced at 7·5 cm (3 ins) apart. Mint is an accommodating herb, growing well in all sorts of soils and in shade or sunshine. Let it grow for a year before you start picking young shoots for boiling with new potatoes and green peas or for mint sauce. After the first pickings in June and July, keep mint well watered in dry summer weather so that plenty of fresh new growth is made for cutting later on. These shoots may be dried or frozen. Mint does well in pots or old plastic buckets. If you are buying a pot for mint growing, a 22-cm (9-in) diameter pot is the minimum size. Use good garden top soil or Levington Potting Compost. Stand a pot of mint close to the kitchen door; this herb is so often wanted during cooking. If you would like early supplies, put your mint in a greenhouse or cold frame after you have cut off all the dead stems in late autumn. Give water now and then to potted mint in winter; in spring, summer and early autumn water often, and very generously in dry weather. Mint growing in a pot will need replanting within three or four years. Use a sharp knife or a spade to slice off a part of the root system. Replant this part in the pot and with fresh soil or compost. If you are not replanting or giving away the rest of the root system, burn it. It is unlikely to rot down in the small- to medium-sized compost heap of most gardens.

Parsley

Sow seeds in spring or in July. Sprinkle fairly thinly at a depth of no more than 2·5 cm (1 in) in seed drills spaced 30 cm (1 ft) apart or in plant containers (pots, tubs, window-boxes, etc.). Moss Curled is a popular parsley. Thin seedlings so that those left have a few centimetres of space in which to thrive. This is one of the few culinary herbs which do quite well in partial shade. Always keep parsley plants well supplied with water in dry summer weather. Plants run to seed (make flowering stems, flowers, set seeds and then die) in their second year of growth. If you live where winters are usually severe, provide parsley plants with cloche protection in late autumn. If the plants are in containers house them in a greenhouse or well-lighted garden shed from late October until early April. Pick parsley as and when wanted.

Hamburgh parsley

This is sometimes called turnip-rooted parsley although the roots resemble small parsnips rather than turnips. It is grown for its roots but the foliage may also be used as a garnishing if the herb, parsley, is not to hand. Sow and cultivate as parsnips (see p. 86). Leave the roots in the garden as you do parsnips or dig in October and store as carrots (see p. 56). Cook as parsnips. Hamburgh parsley is not well known and I suggest you try just a short row to see if you like it. I prefer parsnips!

Sage

Start off with a young bush of broad-leaved (non-flowering) English sage. Wait at least a year before starting to pick foliage as and when it is to be used int the kitchen. Foliage for drying and storing may be cut from well-established sage bushes in May and again in August.

Thyme

Among the many thymes, Common Thyme, also known as Garden Thyme and Black Thyme, is usually grown in the kitchen garden. It is a low growing, perennial shrub. Start off with seeds sown in the manner of parsley. When thinning the seedlings allow each young plant about 30 cm (1 ft) of space in the row. A 25-cm (10-in) diameter pot will take two or three thyme plants. When these look far too packed, dig out two of them. You can replant them in other containers. Cut sprigs for use as they are wanted. For dried thyme cut sprigs before the tiny pale lilac flowers open in late spring or in August.

Kale

This is a brassica grown as greens in winter and early spring. Most popular is the Scottish sort called Curly Kale, which is more important to the gardener living in colder parts of Britain than to southern gardeners who grow the more productive but not quite as hardy sprouting broccolis (see p. 48). Tall Green Curled attains a height of about 90 cm (3 ft); in windy areas, the shorter Dwarf Green Curled should be chosen. Sow seeds in the brassica seed bed in April (see pp. 41–2), move plants to a nursery bed in May and set them out in June or early July. Grow kale plants alongside a row of peas which will be picked and the plants pulled up some time in July, leaving plenty of room for the kale. Hoe occasionally to keep down weeds; only in a very dry summer is it necessary to water the plants. First edible portion to be gathered is the cluster of tender leaves at the tops of kale plants; removing this encourages side shoots to grow in the leaf axils. Pick these shoots for cooking when they are a few centimetres long. After all the shoots have been gathered, dig up the plants, chop them in pieces and add to the compost pile.

Kohlrabi

More popular in Germany than here, Kohlrabi looks like a cross between a turnip and a cabbage and is a member of the brassica tribe (as is the turnip) but while the turnip is a swollen root, kohlrabi is a swollen stem. This sits like a large bulb just above the soil surface with leaves sprouting from it. The skin colour of kohlrabi can be light green or mauve, depending on whether you grow a green kohlrabi such as White Vienna or a purple one such as Purple Vienna. This is a very easy vegetable to grow. Sow seeds at any time between late March and mid July. Sprinkle fairly thinly in 2·5-cm (1-in) deep drills spaced 30 cm (1 ft) apart. Always flood seed drills with water before sowing if the soil is dry in late spring and summer. Thin seedlings to 15 cm (6 in) apart as soon as you can handle them. Always keep the plants well supplied with water in dry spells and use the hoe with great care when weeding. A kohlrabi wounded by the hoe splits and will also split if attacked by slugs when at the seedling stage. Kohlrabi grows almost as fast as summer turnips. Pull for use when no larger than a cricket ball; older, larger kohlrabi can be tough. Some gardening writers say that kohlrabi can be stored in October in the same way as carrots (see p. 56). They are probably right. I do not do this. I grow a short row for freezing in September when the kohlrabi is still young and tender. Very small kohlrabi may be blanched, cooled and frozen whole; larger 'bulbs' should be diced. Apart from slug troubles, the only other pest likely to harm kohlrabi plants is Club Root (see p. 46).

Leek

The leek is a very valuable member of the onion tribe. It is exceptionally hardy and therefore needs no storing. Leeks come into their own when the last onions in store are petering out in late winter. Not only can they play the part of ordinary onions in soups, stews and casseroles, but they may also be served as a second vegetable like cabbage or eaten cold (after boiling) with oil and vinegar. Although the flavour of leeks is decidedly oniony, it is mild. There are easy and complicated ways of growing leeks and I grow the best leeks on our allotment site. Dig the soil, rake level and sow a row of seeds in late March or during the first week of April or as soon as the ground is workable. Make the seed drills 2·5 cm (1 in) deep, sprinkle the seeds quite thickly in them and cover by scuffling with your boots or by using a rake. Always rake around afterwards so that things look neat and remove any largish stones. Keep the weeds down as soon as the seedlings show and water during the summer if the soil is dry. Use a hand fork to dig up the seedlings and select as many of the larger ones as you will need. Ground well-dressed with garden compost for the previous season's winter greens makes a good place for the leek bed. Have the ground dug and raked level beforehand. Now put a garden line in position and make holes with a cabbage dibber 7·5–10 cm (3–4 ins) deep and 15–20 cm (6–8 ins) apart alongside the line. If you are planting several rows space them at 30 cm (12 ins) apart. Now drop a leek seedling into each dibber hole and fill the holes with water. Further cultivation consists simply of hoeing occasionally to prevent weed growth. Only in a very dry summer should it be necessary to water leek plants. If some leeks are still in the ground during April and they are in your way because you want to use the ground for something else, dig them up with a garden fork, do not shake the soil from the roots and replant them in a trench in an out-of-the-way spot from which you can take a few when they are wanted for use. Young leek foliage can be rinsed, chopped finely and added to soups; do not use the old, outer tough leaves. I have grown Lyon, Marble Pillar and Musselburgh and found them equally good.

Lettuce

There are several different types of lettuce – cabbage, cos and loose-leaf, with the cabbage sorts subdivided into the butterheads (with smooth leaves) and the crispheads (with puckered leaves). There are varieties for sowing at different times of the year, too. I think I can make things easier if I explain which varieties I grow and like. For sowing between early April and July I invariably choose Unrivalled, sometimes referred to as Unrivalled (white-seed) to distinguish it from Unrivalled (black-seeded) and a medium-sized cabbage, butterhead type. I quite often sow seeds of the cabbage crisphead lettuce Webbs Wonderful in mid to late April. This large, handsome lettuce is deservedly popular among gardeners. If I wish to grow a few cos lettuces, too, I choose either Little Gem, Lobjoits Green Cos or Paris White. According to lettuce fanciers, Little Gem is the best flavoured of all lettuces. It is a small, compact lettuce intermediate between cabbage lettuce and larger, more upright cos sorts, of which Lobjoits Green and Paris White are typical. If you want a quick-maturing lettuce for sowing in a frame or under cloches in February or March, I suggest the butterhead cabbage variety May Queen. If you have seeds of May Queen over after a winter sowing, keep them for sowing again in July, and cover the plants with cloches in late September. I do not guarantee you tightly hearted lettuces in late October or November but at least there will be lettuce foliage for the salad bowl at a time when garden lettuce is a rarity. With luck there may even be lettuce foliage to serve with cold turkey on Boxing Day.

The secret of success with lettuce is to keep the plants growing quickly but without forcing them in any way. Thus, it is not wise to sow lettuce in the open garden until the soil is warming up. This will be some time in April and I make my first sowing of Unrivalled at the same time as sowing most of my brassicas (see pp. 41–2). The lettuce seeds are sown in exactly the same way as brassicas and in the same bed. Some time in May the seedlings are large enough to handle easily and I move them to their growing quarters in soil which received garden compost for the potato or the cabbage crop the previous season. I use a short length of bamboo cane as the planting tool and set the seedlings at about 25 cm (10 ins) apart, with the same distance between rows. Plant lettuce seedlings at the depth at which they were growing in the seed bed but plant firmly, and never plant out lettuce in dry soil. A lawn sprinkler left in action for an hour or so will wet the soil well.

Sparrows can wreak havoc on lettuce seedlings and plants. I have to protect mine by pushing short pieces of bamboo here and there alongside the rows and then linking the pieces of bamboo with several strands of black cotton. Do not use nylon thread. An inquisitive young sparrow can strangle itself in thread.

The cultivation of cabbage lettuce consists solely of preventing weeds and applying water when necessary. Straw or lawn mowings are useful mulches for lettuce, provided that your garden or allotment is not plagued by slugs. Cos lettuces are supposed to be self folding. Grow them as cabbage lettuce but take my tip – it pays to tie them rather loosely when they are approaching the hearting up stage. Use raffia or soft string (known to gardeners as 'fillis' – not Phyllis!). Tied cos lettuces are always well-hearted. The first lettuces from an April sowing will be ready for use in July. Lettuces do not retain their pristine appearance and quality for long so sow again towards the end of May or early in June for more lettuces in August and September. Sow the seeds fairly thinly where the plants are to grow. Thin seedlings out to about 25 cm (10 ins) apart when they are fairly small. You may care to try Continuity if you think the family would take to a butterhead with green and brown foliage. Some folk rave over it. It's a variety that stands up well to any hot weather we may have in our strange summers. Salad Bowl is a loose-leaf lettuce. Grow it as ordinary cabbage lettuce but instead of cutting the lettuce, pull leaves from plants here and there in the manner of gathering spinach.

Marrows (Vegetable Marrow, Squash and Pumpkin, p. 124)

Melon

The melon is a useful frame or cloche summer crop for the south of England gardener. If you live elsewhere, ask around but it's worth trying yourself anyway. Choose a suitable variety for cloches and frames. Ha-Ogen, Sweetheart and Honey Drip are newer melons and are my particular choice. Good older sorts are Tiger and Charentais or Canteloupe selections – Dutch Net and No Name. Sow as for cucumbers to be grown in a greenhouse or in a garden frame (see pp. 64ff.). If the greenhouse is heated a sowing in late March will make this crop less chancy if the summer is not all that hot. If you wait until late April before sowing in an unheated greenhouse or in a cold frame (as I do), there is always the possibility (although it is rare) that the summer will be very cool and the melons, forming rather late, will not ripen off well. Melon plants are ready for setting out in their growing positions when they have made five or six *true* leaves. Although the melon is not as greedy a feeder as its relative the cucumber, it does require good, fertile soil conditions with exceptionally good drainage. Before planting melons I spread a mulch of garden compost over the site to be cloched or over the bed in the garden frame. To ensure very free drainage I plant melons on a slight hump – made by drawing the compost (using a garden rake) toward the centre of the row or frame. To prevent Stem Rot disease I plant so that the top 1·25 cm ($\frac{1}{2}$ in) or so of the soil ball protrudes above the bed. I also sink a clay or plastic flowerpot into the ground and alongside each plant. Water and any liquid feeds can be applied via the pots. This way of watering rules out any chance of water causing stem rot at the base of the melon plants. Allow each plant 60 cm (2 ft) of row space in a cloched row; 60 sq cm (2 sq ft) in garden frames. Put cloches in position or the frame light on the frame immediately after planting. If you watered well at planting time no water may be needed by the plants for about a week.

It is then, too, that you start pruning the plants. The first pruning is simply to pinch out the central growing point of each plant, causing the plants to make side shoots. On a plant growing in the centre of a small garden frame you can leave four side shoots. Stop any surplus shoots when they have made three leaves.

Guide the four shoots you are retaining to the four corners of the frame; then stop them by pinching off the growing tips. Plants under cloches need only two shoots. Stop any surplus shoots after three leaves and stop the two laterals you are retaining when each is about 60 cm (2 ft) long. The plants will now make many sublateral shoots and you will see many flowers; so that bees and other flying insects may transfer ripe pollen from male flowers to the female flowers, prop up the frame light on warm sunny days or take away a cloche. Keep the plants supplied with water. How much and when to water is something you have to calculate. Final pruning occurs when each plant is bearing two or three fruits about the size of small chicken eggs. Retain only three or four fruits, each on a separate sublateral. Raise the small fruits you are retaining very gently on to pieces of tile, slate or wood or on to inverted flowerpots to prevent the swelling melons from being nibbled by slugs or damaged by soil fungi. Cut back sublaterals to the *second leaf* beyond each small melon; prune back all other growths to the *second leaf* beyond the original main laterals. Continue watering. You may, if you wish, feed now and then with diluted manure water (see p. 66). In a very bright, hot spell, fleck some whitewash over the frame light or cloches or drape old net curtaining over the glass. Always remove shading as soon as the weather changes. In very hot weather the frame light may be propped up a little or a cloche taken away. As soon as a melon stops swelling, stop watering and feeding the plant, otherwise your melons may burst. Cut melons when their delicious ripe odour guides your nose to them. Handle them like eggs: they bruise easily.

Mint (see Herbs, p. 72)

Mustard and cress

This is rarely considered a garden crop but is grown instead in a greenhouse or in the home itself. Do not try to grow mustard and cress in over-cold or over-hot atmospheres; 10–16°C (50–60°F) are suitable temperatures. You need seeds of White Mustard and either Plain or Curled Cress. Sowings are usually made between November and March in seed boxes, flowerpots or bulb bowls. Use a soil-less compost such as Levington Seed or Levington Potting. Cress is slower growing than mustard, therefore sow cress seeds three days before mustard. Firm the compost, water well using a very fine rose on the can and sow fairly thickly on the surface of the compost. Do not cover with compost. Instead, firm the seeds into the moist compost. Stand the containers in a dark place or cover them with several thicknesses of brown paper. Immediately the seeds have germinated take the containers into full light. Water carefully but only if you consider it necessary. Cut the crop when the seedlings are 5–7 cm (2–3 ins) high, which is about a fortnight from sowing. I never like to mention a proprietary gadget because it so often goes off the market, but Suttons have been selling their Mustard and Cress 'farms' for many years. I have seen several kids really enjoying them; they are just the thing to introduce a child to growing home food crops – and the crop is really good.

Onions

Although there are other sorts of onions, those commonly grown in our kitchen gardens and on our allotments are salad onions, maincrop onions and pickling onions.

Unless the ground is infected with Onion White Rot fungus, about which more later, the growing of salad onions is simplicity itself. White Lisbon is the popular variety. Seed may be sown at any time between late March and early September. Just make 2·5-cm (1-in) deep seed drills spaced at 30 cm (1 ft) apart and sprinkle seeds liberally in them. Cover with soil and tread lightly if the soil is loose and puffy. Use a rake to leave the bed neat. Start pulling the larger onions for salads as soon as the young plants are of sufficient size for use. Do not leave the onions to get fat, tough and 'hot'. Do not try to pull salad onions out of dry ground, otherwise the foliage will come away in your hand and the onion bulblets will remain firmly embedded in the dry soil. Broken onion foliage is an invitation to female onion flies to pay an unwelcome call! More about this pest later. Do not expect late summer/early autumn sown onions to be ready for salad use until the following May and June. In a very severe winter expect to lose most or all of the onion seedlings unless you hurriedly protect them with cloches. In very cold parts of the country it would be wiser to sow in drills spaced only 15 cm (6 ins) apart and to cover the seedlings with cloches in late October.

While salad onions are grown for a supply of immature mildly flavoured bulblets, maincrop onions are large, solid and can be stored for use as they are wanted for cooking between September and April. The old way of growing maincrop onions is to sow seeds of a suitable onion (Giant Zittau and Solidity are reliable varieties) in late August. The seedlings are dug up in the following March, sorted through and the stronger ones replanted in good, fertile soil. Alternatively, seeds of varieties such as Ailsa Craig and Bedfordshire Champion are sown in early spring as are salad onions. The seedlings are thinned out once or twice (the larger thinnings being eaten as 'spring' or salad onions). After the final thinning in early July, plants left to grow are spaced from 15 to 20 cm (6–8 ins) apart in the rows.

Some gardeners may still follow either of these practices but all gardeners I know now raise their maincrop onions from 'sets'. These are immature bulbs on sale in winter and early spring and are usually of the variety Stuttgarter Giant (Stuttgarter Riesen). They lead to large, flattish onions of mild flavour and good storing quality. You need 500 gramme (1 lb) sets. When you get them home, tip them out of the bag and spread them on a seed tray or Dutch tray (the give-away trays at greengrocers and in supermarkets). Keep the bulbs in a cool, dry place until planting time.

Always rotate your onions (see Chapter 2). A spot which was well dressed with garden compost for a different crop in the previous season should be chosen. If you have not already dug the soil, do it before setting the garden line in position for the planting of the first row of sets. If the soil is workable, sets may be planted in March. Usually one has to wait until early April. There are two ways of planting onion sets. If the ground were dug recently and if the soil is light, all you need do is push sets into the loose soil between 15–20 cm (6–8 ins) apart. If the soil is on the heavy side or was dug some time back, use a draw hoe to make 2·5-cm (1-in) deep, narrow drills. Plant the sets in the drills. Leave a good 30 cm (1 ft) between the rows so that you will be able to get in among the onions and hoe without damaging them. If you know that local birds invariably tug at dry foliage on onion sets and shallots in a search for nesting material, it will pay you to cut off all excessive dry foliage before planting. I replant any immediately I notice the bulbs on the surface of the ground. Hoe occasionally to prevent weeds and give plenty of water in long spells of dry weather.

Onion sets are prone to a disorder called Saddleback. This splitting of the base of the bulbs can occur between May and early August, due to lack of water at the roots which checks growth. When water in the form of rain arrives the bulbs burst. The gardener does not discover the trouble until bulbs are harvested. Sometimes the splitting of the bases is not severe and although the onions will not store, they can at least be used in the kitchen. Where severe splitting occurs fungal infections also start and the bulbs rot.

During July or August the foliage of maincrop onions changes from green to yellow. The foliage should also topple on to the ground. Here and there a plant remains upright and the gardener has to bend it over gently. In a cool, wet summer the foliage of most onions may remain obstinately upright and stay green instead of turning yellow and shrivelling. If this happens you should bend down the foliage of onions grown from sets or raised from seed sown the previous autumn during mid August. For seed sown in spring, bend the recalcitrant foliage soilwards in early September. To hasten the ripening off of onions in a wet summer, it is also helpful when you bend over the foliage to plunge a garden fork into the ground near the onions and lift it upwards so that many of the onion roots are snapped. Only well-ripened onions will keep well in store. Harvesting the onions means that you simply lift the bulbs off the ground. If by mid September the bent over foliage of your onions is still quite green, dig up the plants and dry them off as best you can. If there is still rain about this may mean spreading out the bulbs on the greenhouse staging, in a cold frame or under cloches. Laying the onions on sacks in the garden is another way of drying them off. As soon as rain threatens roll up the sacks and cart the onions under cover. Always take the onions indoors each evening. Complete the drying process after harvesting. Just tie the onions in bunches and hang them in a sunny position somewhere in the garden. Most of the onions will have shrivelled, brown foliage; a few will still have foliage which is partly green and yellow. Only when all the foliage is brown and brittle are the onions ready for storing. In the meantime onions will be needed for cooking in July, and can be taken for immediate use even though they are not ready for storing. If you have any onions with thickish necks (thick foliage immediately above the onion bulb) use these first as they do not store well.

To prepare well-dried onions for store, rub each onion between your fingers to remove dead roots and *loose* foliage. How you store your onions is up to you. They can be placed in single or

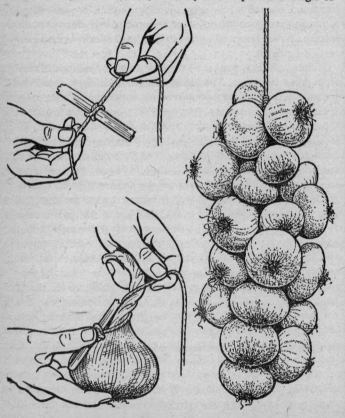

double layers in Dutch trays or hung up in discarded nylon stockings or tights. My own preference is for ropes of onions, so that you can see at a glance if an onion has started to rot or to make premature new foliage. When this happens bulbs soften rapidly and are unfit for use. There are several ways of roping onions. The sketch shows the easy way I rope mine. Where you store your onions is very important. The place must be light, airy, cool but frost-free. An unheated bedroom or lean-to, a garden shed or garage are places which come to mind.

For pickling onions the shallot is usually grown. Shallots may also replace maincrop onions in cooked dishes. To grow shallots you start off with sets. The usual amount to buy and plant is 500 gramme (1 lb). There are red-skinned and yellow-skinned shallots, and the flesh of both sorts is white. Buy your shallots in winter and plant them as soon as soil conditions permit in March or April in the same way as onion sets. Hoe among the plants to keep weeds at bay; watering is seldom necessary. As with onions, shallots almost sit on top of the ground, so when using a hoe draw the soil away from the swelling bulbs and not towards them. With onion sets it is the sets which you plant that swell and produce a single (occasionally a twin) large onion; with shallots, the original mother bulb splits. The segments swell to form clusters of several shallots, which are dug in July or August when the foliage is starting to change from green to yellow. Spread the clusters (as dug) on sacks in full sun. Take under cover if there is a chance of rain. When the shallots are dry and the foliage brown and brittle, tease the clusters apart, rub the bulbs through your fingers to rid them of dead roots, dry soil and *loose* foliage. Pickle soon or store in trays, stockings or tights.

If you have recently taken over a weedy garden or allotment or dug up the lawn to make room for more food crops, your onion seedlings may well receive the attentions of wireworms. Because their natural diet of grass roots has been removed the wireworms make do with whatever is around – namely, the roots of your onions and other vegetables. Affected young onion plants turn yellow and often die. If they are dug up their roots appear to have been shorn off. The roots of onion sets and of shallots are also liable to attack but the damage is seldom serious. The most common trouble with onion growing is damage to seedlings by Onion Fly larvae. Eggs are laid in the soil close to the plants during May; grubs hatch and feed on the roots of the onion plants. Foliage of the plants yellows and plants die. This is a worry I have not had, but precautions should be taken when thinning onions or pulling salad onions similar to those taken to prevent Carrot Fly damage to young carrots (see p. 55). Onion White Rot, commoner than it should be, can attack all members of the onion tribe and is usually caused by a failure on the part of the gardener to rotate his onion bed round the garden or allotment. The old way of growing onions (invariably from seeds) was to sow in a very rich bed devoted year after year to onions. In 1841 White Rot fungus appeared in Britain and it thrives where onions continue to be grown on or near the same patch of ground. Gardeners who do not rotate their onions may be lucky for many years. Then, suddenly, in May or June, the onion plants start to go yellow and to wilt. When the plants are dug up the base of the swelling bulbs is soft; there may also be some fluffy mould present. Bulbs left in the soil turn brown and rot. Burn all affected bulbs and give up growing onions on or near that part of the garden or allotment. With luck, the disease may not have got established in other parts of the garden or plot. If it has, stop growing onions for a few years. The salad onion White Lisbon is particularly susceptible; maincrop onion Bedfordshire Champion is reputed to be somewhat resistant to Onion White Rot.

Parsley (see Herbs, p. 73)

Parsnip

This is strictly a winter vegetable. Not everybody likes parsnips so check on how many of the family enjoy them before deciding whether to sow a couple of rows or none at all. Which variety you sow depends on your soil. If you have a good depth of soil choose long-rooted sorts like Improved Hollow Crown. Where the soil is shallow and on top of clay, chalk or gravel, I suggest you choose any seedsman's 'Intermediate', a shorter-rooted parsnip. Avonresister is another parsnip which does not make a really long root and is never all that large so the plants do not need as much space in the row as other sorts. Choose a part of the garden which was dressed with garden compost in the previous season or the year before that. Parsnips need good, fertile soil but not a soil which has pockets of manure or compost in it, otherwise the roots 'fork'. That is to say, instead of getting a nice straight parsnip, you dig roots which are fanged and so pretty useless to the cook. Parsnip seed may be sown as soon as you can get out into the garden without bringing a great part of it back indoors on your boots! I used to be able to sow in late February but now I wait till early April. Let me explain why: the soil is cold in February and March. Parsnip seeds take quite a time to germinate and if you sow in cold soil, annual weeds germinate before the parsnip seeds and smother them. True, you may read elsewhere that you can get over this problem by sowing radish seeds along with and in the same seed drills as parsnips, because radish seeds, being quick to germinate, will appear long before the parsnip seedlings and the gardener can use the hoe around the radishes and keep down weed seedlings. Practice proves the theory impracticable. Radish seeds sown in cold soil are not quick to germinate. After germination the weather is still cold; in cold conditions radishes swell slowly and radishes which do not grow rapidly are woody and pretty inedible. On top of this, when pulling radishes for use, one has to get them out from among the parsnip seedlings. These are loosened and one wishes one had not attempted the growing of two different vegetables in the same seed row. Sow parsnip seeds in 2·5-cm (1-in) deep drills spaced 30 cm (1 ft) apart. Sow the seeds fairly thickly and, if there is a wind blowing, water the seed drill. When the water drains away there is sticky mud in the drill. I hold the seed packet close to the ground, take out pinches of seed, sprinkle the seeds in a small part of the wet drill, cover with a handful of dry soil and proceed to sow more seeds. If you try sowing parsnip seed in windy weather without doing this, you will find the seeds blowing like confetti around the garden or allotment. Scuffle loose soil over the drills to cover them, using your boots or a rake. Rake all level and mark the rows with plant labels, showing the name of the variety sown. A week or two after the seedlings show, thin them out to leave strong seedlings at 5-7·5 cm (2–3 ins) apart. I find an onion hoe comes in handy to do this job. A month or so later thin again to leave plants 15–20 cm (6–8 ins) apart. Further cultivation consists only of hoeing carefully occasionally to prevent weed growth. Parsnips are quite hardy. Just leave them in the ground until you wish to dig a few for use between December and March. The approved way of digging parsnips is to use a spade to make a trench alongside them so that undamaged roots may be pulled out of the ground. I find it easier to push a garden fork into the soil on either side of a parsnip and to ease the fork upwards. The skin of a parsnip is sometimes damaged but this is of little consequence when the vegetable is to be used at once. If some of the crop is still in the ground in early spring, dig up the roots and store in a trench in the way suggested for leeks (see p. 76). Use any remaining parsnips before April because as soon as new foliage shows the centre core of a parsnip toughens and the roots are past their best.

Parsnip Canker, the only worry you may meet in the growing of this root crop, is a disorder and not a disease. It is brought about by the cracking of the skin of the swelling root. Fungi and bacteria invade the cracks and in badly infected cases the parsnips have deep reddish-brown patches and rotted flesh. More usually parsnips are mildly affected and the browned pieces are cut off by the cook during preparation of the vegetable. Wireworms and other soil inhabitants are often accused of making small holes in parsnips and thus permitting entry of fungi and bacteria. It is far more likely that the trouble originates when parsnip plants are not well watered in dry summer weather. When heavy rain falls later the skin of the parsnips cracks, in the same way that tomatoes crack when water has been denied them. When Avonresister was introduced several years ago it was thought that this new parsnip was the answer to Canker. Unfortunately, it only resists Canker up to a point; Tender and True is another parsnip which shows some resistance.

Peas

Garden peas are divided into two groups: those with smooth seeds (called round-seeded) and those with wrinkled seeds (called wrinkled-seeded or marrowfats). The marrowfats are supposed to be the best for flavour although this depends so much on your own taste buds. Round-seeded sorts were always hardier but there are now hardy marrowfats, too. There are Early, Second Early and Maincrop peas, varying in height from just over 30 cm (1 ft) to 1·8 m (6 ft) tall. Tall peas are not favoured these days because it is difficult to find 2-m (7-ft) tall pea sticks; they have to be bought. If all this sounds complicated, I am not surprised. Let me make things easier for you.

You may, if you wish, simply stick to one variety – and I strongly recommend Kelvedon Wonder – for sowing between late March and mid June for successional cropping. Peas, unlike runner beans from which one picks pods over a period of a couple of months, crop for only about two weeks, which is why (when one has the ground) peas are sown successionally.

Pea plants need well drained soil and plenty of moisture in it. Do not sow peas in ground recently dressed with garden compost or rotted dung. In the vegetable rotation, peas can follow potatoes or winter greens. Although a very hardy pea like Feltham First can be sown in the open ground or under cloches in late autumn, this is a rare practice. Most gardeners wait until the soil is workable in spring, usually between late March and mid April. Set the garden line in position and with a draw hoe make a 2·5–5 cm (1–2 in) drill 15–20 cm (6–8 ins) wide and flat bottomed. The soil is usually quite moist in early spring but when sowing peas later on always flood the drill with water and sow when it has drained away. The correct way of sowing peas is to space them in two or three rows in the drill with the seeds at about 5–7·5 cm (2–3 ins) apart. I followed this way of pea sowing zealously for more than twenty years. Sometimes results were excellent; sometimes quite a lot of seeds failed to germinate so that I had gaps in the rows, and pea seedlings cannot be transplanted successfully to fill gaps. Now I sow pea seeds thickly and I suggest you do the same. Peas are not the easiest of vegetables to grow and one's first trouble can start immediately after sowing when birds (usually starlings and house sparrows) decide to investigate. When pea seedlings are just showing through the ground birds peck at the green shoots. You have to stop all this nonsense, either by cloche protection or by pushing short lengths of bamboo on either side of the pea row and right up against it. I run two or three strands of black cotton from bamboo to bamboo and then a few strands across the top and over the row, which is 'caged'. Birds do not like feeling cotton as their feet come down towards the ground. The young pea plants take to the cotton as readily as to twiggy brushwood and their tendrils grasp the cotton which I add to later on with strings wound at intervals of several centimetres from bamboo to bamboo. If the bamboo supports are very short they have to be augmented by some taller canes when the pea plants are growing well. How long the supports need to be depends on the final height of the pea plants. Kelvedon Wonder grows to a height of between 45–60 cm (18–24 ins) and 90-cm (3-ft) bamboo canes are needed. Keeping down weeds between rows of peas is easy. (By the way, if you are sowing another row of peas next to ones already sown, leave the gap between the rows equal to the final height of the peas. If you go in for tall growing peas you will understand why many gardeners say they do not grow peas because the plants take up so much space. But the space between rows can be utilized [see Chapter 2].) But back to weeds. There will also be weed seedlings among the young pea plants, which have to be hand-weeded. Later you may see a tall weed here and there among fully-grown pea plants, which may be cut down or left where it is. Do not tug it out of the ground or you will loosen roots of several pea plants.

Never let pea plants get dry at the roots. It is this continual need for water which makes allotment pea growing risky if the allotment site is a long way off and the weather dry. Because there is more moisture in the ground in spring and early summer than later on (unless the summer is a wet one), few allotment-holders sow peas after mid April. A sprinkler must be left on for a few hours so that the soil is really well soaked. If you apply water with a can, remember that you must keep on watering (perhaps daily) until rain falls. If you don't, the soil will dry and harden and your pea plants will sicken. Straw or lawn mowings are useful mulching materials to spread around rows of peas in May or early June. If all has gone well your peas will flower and set lots of pods. Pick pods when they are well filled with sweet young peas. Old pods contain starchy, tougher peas. If you wish to have peas for the freezer grow a special row or pick a batch of pods when the peas are at the peak of condition.

Peas are legumes and have bacteria in nodules on their roots. The bacteria manufacture nitrogen from the atmosphere. Although some of the roots will be pulled up when you tug at the haulm (growth above ground) after the last picking of peas and cart the plants to the compost pile, you can increase the soil nitrogen content by hoeing or digging in the pea roots. I find the hoe the better tool. It cuts through annual weeds in the pea rows. This nitrogen supply should be available to other garden subjects immediately. If you have set out plants of brussels sprouts or sprouting broccoli a few weeks earlier alongside the rows of peas, the young plants of these brassicas will be able to make use of the nitrogenous salts.

Mildew is a common disease of peas. Pods fail to swell and change from green to brown/black; the foliage changes to yellow and plants die. Prevent mildew by ensuring that plants always have sufficient moisture at the roots. The Pea Moth can be a great nuisance, especially to peas grown in southern England, where the moths are more plentiful. Female Pea Moths lay eggs at around flowering time and the grubs from the eggs bore into the small pods and devour the peas within. After an attack the gardener finds many of his pea pods spoilt by maggots. Usually only a few peas in each pod are maggoty; sometimes every pea is affected. The maggots, meanwhile, drop on to the soil and enter it to hibernate in cocoons. When the soil is dug many of the cocoons are exposed and the garden bird population devours them. I have had trouble with Pea Moth damage. I noticed that it occurred when I had not kept the plants very moist during the flowering period. I now water well and often when the plants are flowering if the weather is dry and I also spray the plants with cold water occasionally. These simple preventives appear to stop Pea Moth trouble. Kelvedon Wonder and Foremost are reputed to be less susceptible to Pea Moth than most other varieties. Pea Moth damage is also less likely in pods from sowings made in late March or early April than in pods from later sowings.

Potatoes

The potato reached Britain from South America in the sixteenth century. The Irish, because they had little else in the way of food, took readily to the new, foreign food. Folk in Britain thought potato-eating a rather unpleasant habit. Churchmen pointed out that the potato does not figure in Holy Writ and this vegetable was not widely grown in England, Scotland and Wales until the nineteenth century. Potato varieties are divided into three groupings: First Early, Second Early and Maincrop, which gardeners often refer to as 'Lates'. All are planted at the same time and Good Friday is the traditional planting date. But where winter lingers on, it pays to delay potato planting until late April, as frost blackens and kills the young foliage; the tubers produce more foliage but the check to growth can lead to a lower yield. First Early varieties bulk up quickly and there should be 'new' potatoes for eating with garden peas by late June. Garden- or allotment-grown new potatoes are a luxury then and although no more than 500 grammes (1 lb) of potatoes (which will be on the small side, too) can be expected from each root, the gardener who has them is envied by those forced to pay high prices in the shop. Plants of First Earlies are dug almost daily throughout July and August, and the weight per root increases as the summer progresses, yielding 1 kg (2 lb) and 1·5 kg (3 lb) in July and, if the soil is good and has been kept moist in dry weather, 2 kg (4 lb) to 3·5 kg (7 lb) in August. Even heavier yields are possible from soils which have been built up from the fertility point of view. First Earlies tend to die in late August and early September, and remaining plants should be dug as soon as the haulm (top growth) is brown and dry. By then the skins of the tubers will have set and the potatoes can be used immediately or stored for autumn and early winter use. First Earlies store well until Christmas at least.

Second Earlies and Maincrop have better storing quality. The tubers do not swell as rapidly and the plants are not usually dug until the haulm has died down and is brown and dry (late September or early October). Naturally, the gardener who runs out of First Earlies in August starts digging his Second Earlies then, even though the haulm may be bright green and lush. The weight of crop from Second Earlies and Maincrop should be higher than that from First Earlies, because the digging of the latter starts when the tubers are very immature. Here are some popular varieties:

First Early	Second Early	Maincrop
Arran Pilot*	Catriona*	Arran Banner*
Duke of York	Craig's Royal*	Desirée*
Epicure	Great Scot*	Golden Wonder*
Home Guard*	Maris Peer*	King Edward
Sharpe's Express	Maris Piper*	Majestic*
Ulster Chieftain*	Pentland Dell*	Pentland Crown*

* Immune against Wart Disease (see p. 99).

As you can see, the choice of varieties is wide. Flavour is important in vegetables when you are growing your own. Among the First Earlies, Duke of York has a reputation for flavour. Arran Pilot hasn't, yet I have grown it season after season for more than twenty-five years. I shall continue to grow it, too. My work has involved growing and tasting over one hundred different potato varieties and few have the cropping potential and flavour of Arran Pilot. There is little point in growing a Second Early and few gardeners do so. Among good-storing Maincrops, steer clear of King Edward unless you know that it crops well in your part of the world. Soil conditions must be perfect for King Edward, best known potato of all with a reputation for good cooking quality and for storing well until June. Majestic does well in light soils and the flavour is at its best in late winter. Arran Banner and Pentland Crown are noted for good cropping, although you may consider them somewhat poorly flavoured. Golden Wonder is noted as being the best-flavoured potato of all and also a poor cropper! There just isn't room in the average garden or allotment for many rows of potatoes and unless you have a really large garden, my advice is that you forget Second Earlies and Maincrops and stick to First Earlies. As I have said before, the tubers keep well until Christmas at least and if potatoes are eaten daily in your home the entire crop will have been cooked and enjoyed by then.

To grow potatoes you need 'seed'. 'Seed' in potato growing means tubers produced by farmers in parts of Britain where virus diseases are not endemic. Certified (virus-free, etc.) seed potatoes of a few varieties are on sale in garden shops and in chain stores during the winter. A better range is offered by a few mail order seed firms but at prices far higher than those in your local shops, due to present-day high carriage charges. Buy seed tubers as soon as you spot them on sale; do not wait until April and wander from town to town seeking any tubers still about. Never plant potatoes bought for eating, as they are liable to be carriers of virus troubles and other nasty potato diseases. The plot-holder who plants ware (potatoes sold for eating) is an ignorant gardener and his action can introduce killer diseases to potatoes on the entire allotment site.

The potato plant needs good drainage, lots of nourishing food, plenty of water when the tubers are swelling and sufficient space for good development. This vegetable is quite frequently recommended as a 'cleaning crop' for new gardens and allotments, because the haulm is a smotherer and will make life unbearable for perennial and annual weeds. In practice, things can go wrong. If couch grass (twitch) has been dug in, every small piece of it will throw up new shoots; they can pierce and grow through potato tubers. If the weedy ground (or lawn dug up for vegetable growing) contained wireworms, these will turn to potato roots and tubers as a new source of food. Neglected gardens and allotments usually have a large population of black slugs in the ground. These like nothing better than to gnaw through potato tubers until they resemble a miniature underground railway system! So, when preparing weedy land for potatoes and other vegetables, rid it of weeds and weed roots, bait for wireworms (see Chapter 1), expect to have some holes in your potatoes and do not rely on potato plants doing the work which you have to do yourself. But to return to the tubers you have bought. You can work out about how many to buy by measuring the space you can allot this vegetable, studying the planting distances below and calculating that each 7 kg (14 lb) of seed will average in the region of 60/70 tubers. When you get the tubers home, take them out of the bag gently and stand them (eye-end upwards) in Dutch trays. At the other end of the tuber you will see the remnant of the dried root which linked the tuber to the parent plant. House the trays of tubers in a dry, frost-proof, well-lighted place. Have a look at them occasionally, and take out and burn the rare tuber which shows signs of rot. By planting time all of the tubers will have made short, stubby green or mauve shoots. The ground must be dug beforehand. How you plant potatoes is up to you; the manner of cultivation is your choice too. Sometimes the methods of one part of Britain are not suitable for other parts. By all means watch what other local gardeners do if you are just starting gardening. Here is how I plant and cultivate to get my own impressive crops. First of all the soil must be workable, and you may have to wait a week or more for sun and wind to dry it. I mark the rows with a garden line for straightness. Because my soil is light I can use a potato dibber for planting. If your soil has a high clay content, take out 15–20-cm (6–8-in) wide, 12–15-cm (5–6-ins) deep trenches, using a draw hoe or a spade. My dibber holes are about 15 cm (6 ins) deep so that the tops of the tubers are about 7·5 cm (3 ins) below the soil surface. Planting distances vary depending on which group of potatoes you are planting.

	Distance between tubers in the row		Distance between rows	
	cm	inches	cm	inches
First Earlies	25–30	10–12	60	24
Second Earlies	30–37	12–15	75	30
Maincrop	37	15	75	30

Plant eye-end upwards. Roots and foliage of potato plants are produced on the shoots at the tops of the tubers and not directly from the tubers themselves. Take care when planting that tender young shoots are not damaged. There is no need to reduce the number of shoots, as is sometimes advised. After planting, fill in the dibber holes or the shallow trenches. When I have a row or two planted I spread garden compost thickly over the whole bed. More potatoes are planted and more compost is spread. If some of the compost looks a bit rough, do not worry; any very rough material can be removed when weeding later, but most will have disintegrated completely by the time Maincrop potatoes are dug. In May or early June I rid the bed of all weeds, either by hand, or, if the garden compost was very well decomposed, I am able to use a Dutch hoe between the rows. The job is so automatic that it gives the mind a very pleasant rest. As soon as dry weather sets in, water often and plentifully. To have the best crops of potatoes on the allotment site involves my hauling 500 kgs ($\frac{1}{2}$ ton) water in 9-litre (2-gallon) cans to my potato plants of a Sunday afternoon! Other plot-holders are aghast when they see me doing this; they are aghast later when they compare my potato crop with their own. The occasional tall weed is pulled up, or cut off if pulling it will disturb a good root of potatoes.

Before being stored, potatoes must be quite dry. In a very hot summer the tubers dry off almost at once if left on top of the ground for a few hours. In a wet summer I spread the tubers in single layers in Dutch trays in the garden, which are taken under cover each evening and in the daytime, too, if rain starts. When it comes to storing I rub off any dry soil adhering to the tubers and separate them into medium to large (to be stored), smalls (to be used soon) and damaged (to be used immediately). Damage may mean some slug damage; more often (with me) it means that I have stuck the fork tines right through a huge tuber. Any very tiny tubers are added to the compost heap; always take out these chats when digging potatoes, otherwise potato plants appear like weeds among carrots, peas and beans in the following summer. Any tubers which have a part of the skin green in colour are also used at once. The green areas are cut away when the tubers are being peeled. Potatoes which are very green are not edible. The dry medium to large tubers are placed in double layers in Dutch trays, covered with sheets of newspaper (to exclude light) and stacked in the spare bedroom, or some other convenient, cool, place or in the cellar. An outhouse is a good spot, so is a garden shed, provided that you deal with any mouse problem and spread straw or old sacks over and around the potatoes if the winter is a very cold one. For many gardeners there are few, if any, potatoes to store. If one is growing a host of different vegetables, there is precious little room for lots of potato rows in our modern small gardens. Even an allotment, although it may look large when

The author spreading a few shovels of garden top-soil over each layer
of wastes

Compost made by the American Black Sheet method. The polythene
sheeting is secured with scrap iron poles or other weighty objects

Chinese artichokes

Globe artichokes

Jerusalem artichokes can grow to a height of 2.5 m (8 ft)

Cauliflower: English Wonder-Reading Giant

Cucumber: Telegraph

Beetroot: Boltardy

Horseradish roots

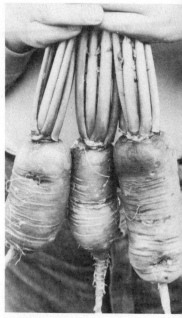

Radish: China Rose

Turnip: Golden Perfection

Blackcurrant: Blacksmith

Blackberries grown on a trellis

Melons grown in a frame

Victoria plums

Gooseberry: Whitesmith

Strawberry: La Sans Rivale

Apple: Sunset

Pear: William's Bon Chrétien

Loganberries

Sunday morning on an allotment site

vacant, does not allow for many rows of potatoes if the gardener is wisely producing other, more expensive-to-buy food crops.

Many gardeners 'earth up' potato rows. This is a useful weeding practice on the farm; but it disturbs potato roots, is back-aching and if badly done can lead to many greened potatoes when an August thunderstorm washes the loose soil hoed up around the potato plants back into the gulley. I see no point in earthing up potatoes as a gardening practice. It originates from Spain, where potatoes, tomatoes and climbing beans are all earthed up to make irrigation channels which are filled with water each morning in summer.

Like all garden plants, the potato has its share of potential troubles. First to start can be *Blackleg*. In June a plant here and there looks stunted with pale green or yellowish leaves. The base of the stem is brown/black and may rot. Dig up and burn affected plants. The cause of this bacterial disease may be due to poor soil drainage or to the planting of tubers which had started to decay. Another cause is said to be the cutting of large tubers into small sections, which was once a common practice in Britain.

Potato Blight shows as moist brown/black blotches on leaves and stems. The plants rot and the fungal spores often drop to the soil and spread on to the potatoes which also rot. This disease, not to be expected in a dry summer, is a greater hazard in the usually wetter, western half of the country. The preventive measure is to spray potato plants fortnightly between early July and mid September with such fungicides as Bordeaux Mixture, maneb and zineb. A pneumatic sprayer is needed so that the underside of the leaves is well coated with the fungicide as well as the top surface. I have yet to meet a gardener who has taken this commonly advised preventive measure. Usually Blight is not a worry to the home food grower. First Earlies are very seldom affected. Tubers of the Second Early, Maris Piper, are said to resist Blight even when this is on the foliage. Pentland Crown is another relatively new potato which appears to withstand Blight trouble well. If Blight symptoms show on your potatoes it is always wise to dig the crop at once. Sort out and burn all tubers showing brown or rotting patches and the haulms of the plants. Dry all unaffected tubers outdoors before storing them. Go through the trays at least once each week to check if any tubers have started to rot. Remove these and burn them.

Common Scab shows as rough, scurfy scabs on the skin of potatoes. The trouble is only skin deep and in no way affects the eating qualities of the tubers. Do your best to prevent this blemish by growing the plants in very fertile soil and do not lime the site reserved for the current season's potato bed. Common Scab is particularly apparent where the soil is very sandy or gravelly. Planting seed tubers on a 2·5-cm (1-in) layer of peat, leaf mould or lawn mowings is said to help defeat the fungus which causes Common Scab.

Virus infections usually show as a mottling and curling of the foliage coupled with a dwarfing effect of the sick plant. To prevent this trouble always invest in new 'seed' each season. Also, always dig up every tiny tuber when you are lifting roots for use. In spring, dig up any potato plants which come up from small tubers you missed.

Potato plants are also dwarfed if Eelworms are attacking the roots. Later the leaves turn yellow, then brown and plants die. Eelworms are microscopic worm-like creatures which cannot be seen by the naked eye. If you learn, following an inspection by a specialist in plant diseases, that your soil is infected with Potato Root Eelworm, you will have to give up potato growing for several years. To prevent eelworm, plant only certified 'seed', practise crop rotation and apply lots of garden compost to the garden or allotment soil. It is believed that garden compost contains minute predators able to combat eelworms.

Slugs, the worst enemy of the potato grower, are a part of the garden scene and can hardly be considered a great nuisance in gardens which are well drained and which have been well cared for over the years. Digging exposes the slugs to birds, but because of their dark colour, do not expect to notice many of them. Do not attempt to mulch (see Chapter 2) potatoes and other vegetables if you have recently taken over a weedy garden or allotment. Good cultivation sees less and less slug troubles as the seasons go by. In a very wet summer slug damage is common to potatoes and the cook can cut out the damaged portions when preparing the tubers. Never store slug-nibbled potatoes.

The potato varieties list (see p. 93) shows which varieties are immune from Wart Disease. As you will see, relatively few of the potatoes we grow today are likely to be the victims of this rare fungal disease which causes warty outgrowths at the eyes (buds from which shoots arise) of tubers. The outgrowths can also appear on the foliage of plants. The fungus is at first white; it then blackens and leads to rotting of plants and tubers. If you suspect Wart Disease you are bound to report the incident to the appropriate agricultural authority. In England this means the Ministry of Agriculture. All infected plants and tubers must be burnt if the authority confirms Wart Disease. From then on, plant only immune varieties. Preventive measures you can take are to plant only certified seed each spring and to warn less knowledgeable neighbours and fellow plot-holders of the danger of planting ware tubers.

Pumpkins
(see Vegetable Marrow, Squash and Pumpkin, p. 124)

Radishes

Radishes fall into two groups: spring/summer, autumn/winter. Gardeners usually grow only spring/summer sorts. These can be round, half long and long and vary in colour from completely red, red and white and all-white. Some seedsmen offer packets of mixed varieties, or you may prefer to choose from among the varieties offered separately. French Breakfast, a white-tipped, red radish, is popular. Other varieties are equally good. The radish is one of the fastest-growing garden vegetables and because radishes deteriorate rapidly if not pulled and eaten immediately they are fully-grown, small batches of seed have to be sown on and off between mid April and mid August. If the ground is not crumbly, dig it to a depth of about 15–20 cm (6–8 ins) before sowing radish. Rake well after digging and make a 2·5-cm (1-in) deep, 5–7·5-cm (2–3-in) wide seed drill with a draw hoe. If you are sowing more than a single row leave about 30 cm (1 ft) between rows. The radish plants do not need this wide spacing but you will when you are cultivating and gathering the crop. In late spring and summer, flood seed drills with water before sowing and sow fairly evenly and thinly when the water has drained away. Perhaps the best advice I can give on sowing is to suggest that you keep in mind that each plant will need about 2·5 sq cm (1 sq in) of space for its good growth. If you sow too thickly you will have spindly, inedible radishes; if you sow too thinly, you will have gaps in the rows. Do not attempt to transplant radish seedlings. True, seedlings can be transplanted but this checks the speedy growth this vegetable has to make. Gardeners who sow in March are seldom pleased with their resultant crop because the plants have grown so slowly in the cold conditions usually prevailing in that month. Giving two or three closely spaced rows cloche or frame protection in early spring may seem a good idea. I find that so often cloche- and frame-sown radishes tend to make excessive foliage at the expense of succulent radishes. Hoe occasionally to keep down weeds and water well and often in dry weather (a lawn sprinkler is excellent for this). Slugs can be a nuisance to radishes and I advise you to go back to Chapter 1 if radish growing in your garden or allotment is not easy because of regular slug damage.

Start pulling radishes out of the ground for use as soon as they appear large enough. I cannot tell you what size this will be. Radishes vary somewhat in size according to variety. Remember that most radishes get either woolly or tough if not eaten when young; they may also get 'hot'. Long White Icicle is an exception among summer radishes. Because it is larger, this radish takes a week or so longer to grow to full size but when it has reached that point it remains in good condition (as far as its eating quality is concerned) for about a fortnight.

Autumn/winter radishes are large and relatively few gardeners even know about them. Sow seeds during the last two weeks of June; if sown earlier, the plants will almost certainly bolt (make flowering stems) and there will be no radishes. If you sow later there may not be time for the radishes to get to a decent size. The seeds are large and can be sown separately from 5 cm (2 ins) apart in one straight sow in a seed drill no deeper than 2·5 cm (1 in). If you sow more than one row, leave 30 cm (12 ins) between seed drills. Most seedsmen offer China Rose or the round or long forms of Black Spanish. When the seedlings appear use a draw hoe around them to prevent weeds and thin the seedlings to 10 cm (4 ins) apart. Two or three weeks later thin again to leave strong plants from 20 cm (8 ins) apart. Water if the soil gets dry. There will be radishes for use sometime in September and any still in the garden in October may be stored in the same way as carrots in moist sand or peat (see p. 56). Slice them thinly (after peeling) or peel and grate for use in sandwiches, in salads or with cheese.

Rhubarb

This is a vegetable used as a fruit. Unfortunately for its own well-being, because it will grow in any sort of soil and in any position, far too often rhubarb doesn't get decent treatment and becomes a sort of garden Cinderella. But there is no Fairy Godmother to hand in our gardens and neglected rhubarb responds accordingly. I would be ashamed to take home the wispy sticks of rhubarb I see being pulled by far too many other gardeners and plot-holders. Give rhubarb a fair deal and just see how the plants respond with thick sticks 60 cm (2 ft) or more long – in fact, as good as mine.

To grow rhubarb you need crowns (pieces of chunky root with at least one fat bud). Although rhubarb can be raised from seeds, this is not the way most gardeners do things. If a neighbour is renewing a bed of healthy-looking rhubarb there will be crowns aplenty for you. If you buy rhubarb crowns, I strongly advise you to invest in the early variety, Timperley Early. Planting usually takes place in November, but you can plant at any time during the winter provided the soil is workable. Choose an open, sunny site and if the ground has been dug beforehand just take out planting holes 1·2 m (4 ft) apart and sufficiently large so that one crown may be planted easily in each. Leave the pink buds on the crowns just at soil level. Firm well after planting, using your boots and taking care not to step on the pink buds. Now cover the bed (the small area in which the rhubarb crowns have been planted) with a 2·5-cm (1-in) thick layer of garden compost or strawy manure. A similar manure or compost dressing should be spread over the bed each autumn. Weed by hand and water well now and then if the summer is a dry one. Never pull rhubarb during the first season after planting, or you will weaken the crowns. Tidy up the bed in the late autumn, consigning dead leaves and stems to the compost pile. Encourage rhubarb plants to settle down and grow well. During the second spring only pull two or three sticks from each crown; in subsequent years you can pull far more rhubarb from your healthy, strong plants. Stop pulling rhubarb at the Spring Bank Holiday. In September pull a few sticks if wanted for wine making. I do not recommend making rhubarb wine from these old sticks but rhubarb comes in handy if you are short of fruit; if you need 6 kg (12 lb) of apples, for example, and have only 5 kg (10 lb), add 1 kg (2 lb) rhubarb to make up.

Rhubarb crowns gradually disintegrate and produce younger crowns around them. Decide when you feel you ought to dig up the entire bed, choose a few young crowns and replant them in a new bed elsewhere in the garden or allotment. But this is a job for ten years or more ahead.

Rhubarb is healthy stuff. About the only trouble you can have is Crown Rot. The term covers several diseases and leads to a rotting of the crown and death of the entire plant. It can be avoided by always hand weeding around rhubarb and always pulling sticks away cleanly from the base of the plants.

Sage (see Herbs, p. 74)

Salsify and Scorzonera

Both these winter root vegetables are sown in the same way and cultivation is identical. Salsify roots (also known as the Vegetable Oyster because of some fanciful oyster-like flavour) resemble rather small parsnips; Scorzonera (also known as Black Salsify) has a single, thin, black-skinned root. I consider both as rather poor substitutes for parsnip. This must be sheer heresy to cordon bleu chefs and I hope that I shall meet one at a future date and be convinced that I am wrong. Cookery writers who tell us that scorzonera should be cooked whole do not suggest what size of cooking vessel will take 35-cm (15-in) long scorzonera roots with ease! However, by all means try these two vegetables if you have the space and feel so inclined. Sow in 2·5-cm (1-in) deep seed drills spaced at 30 cm (1 ft) apart in April. Cultivate as parsnips (see p. 86) and start lifting roots for use in October or November.

Seakale

This native British plant was at one time plentiful on the south
Devon coast. It is rarely found in gardens or on allotments these
days for two good reasons. Most gardeners do not know this
vegetable at all. Those who do say quite rightly that plants take
up far more space than the return they supply as an edible vegetable. On top of these points, seakale has to be blanched. Although
plants can be raised from seed you will have blanched seakale
years earlier if, like me, you start off with thongs (pieces cut from
the thick roots). Plant these in March in fertile soil and in a sunny
position, using a cabbage dibber to make holes at 30–45 cm (12–18
ins) apart. The flat top of the thongs should be at 1 cm ($\frac{1}{2}$ in)
below the surface of the bed with the slanting end of the thongs
pointed downwards into the ground. Plant firmly and mulch
afterwards with garden compost or strawy manure. Hand weed
(using your fingers or a hand fork) to keep down weeds in
summer, water well in dry spells. Liquid manure feeds may also
be applied (see p. 66). The foliage will die down in late autumn
and you can start the blanching process in November by spreading
autumn leaves or straw to a thickness of about 10 cm (4 ins) over
several plants. Invert large pots, old buckets or boxes over the
plants, weighing them down so that wind does not blow them
away. All light must be excluded. Black polythene film comes in
handy if light can get through intersections in boxes. During
March or early April there will be blanched shoots for use. Use a
sharp knife and go down to below the surface of the soil to cut
tight clusters of blanched shoots. In late April, remove pots,
buckets or boxes and allow the plants to make their usual 45–60
cm (18–24 ins) of top growth. Pinch out all flower buds immediately
you see any, as flowering wastes the energy of the plants. Blanch
more seakale in the following autumn/winter. Older crowns
gradually disintegrate and small crowns form around them as with
rhubarb. When, after five or six years your seakale bed needs
renewal, dig up all the roots in November and replant small
crowns or thongs in a new bed.

Seakale beet

This vegetable, grown for its edible foliage, is also known as Swiss Chard and Silver Beet. All the foliage is eaten. The glossy white midribs may be cooked as real seakale and the green parts of the leaves cooked as spinach. Choose a spot in the garden or on the allotment which was well-manured or composted for potatoes or winter greens during the previous season and take out 2·5-cm (1-in) deep seed drills spaced 35 cm (15 ins) apart during April or May. Sow the seeds fairly thinly and thin out the seedlings to leave strong ones standing 30 cm (1 ft) apart. Hoe to keep down the weeds and water generously in dry weather. Harvest a few leaves from each plant as with spinach (see p. 105). If you have cloches to spare, cover the plants in the autumn and there will be some foliage to pick during winter; even without winter protection they will make new growth during the spring unless killed by exceptionally hard frosts. Pick foliage before the plants throw up flowering stems and sow fresh seed elsewhere for more seakale beet in the summer.

There is a red form of this vegetable called Rhubarb Chard or Ruby Chard, which is also edible and a handsome plant, suited to the flower garden.

Shallots (see Onions, p. 81)

Spinach

True spinach is not easy to grow. Long-Standing Round is a standard variety for sowing between late March and late June. Sow seeds fairly thinly in 2·5-cm (1-in) deep seed drills spaced 30 cm (1 ft) apart. Thin the seedlings to leave them 7 cm (3 ins) apart. If conditions are not right, the plants will 'bolt' instead of making lots of foliage to eat. Good, rich soil and plenty of moisture at the roots are vital with summer spinach.

Long-Standing Prickly (the prickly refers to the seeds and not the foliage) is the standard spinach for 'winter and spring'. Seeds are sown and thinned in July as with summer spinach. If the plants appear to need more space in a few weeks' time, pull up and use every second plant. If the plants are denied water or are not growing in very fertile soil, they remain stunted. I have found that even given first-class growing conditions the plants do not grow large and winter frosts take toll of many of them, and by the spring the few surviving plants are not worth the ground they occupied. Cloche protection might have led to better results.

You may well wonder how so many gardeners grow spinach easily without these problems. Nowadays the gardener usually goes in for the easy-to-grow Perpetual Spinach, which is not really a spinach at all, being a form of beet – as is seakale beet. The bright green leaves are picked in the same way as true spinach. In fact, many gardeners who grow Perpetual Spinach think they are growing an improved sort of ordinary spinach which has none of the drawbacks of round-seeded and prickly-seeded sorts. Spinach Beet is another name for this leaf vegetable. Sow seeds in April in the same way as real spinach. You need quite a long row (say 6 m or 20 ft) to have fairly regular pickings. Thin the seedlings to 20 cm (8 ins) apart. Hoe to prevent weeds and water in dry summer weather. Start picking leaves when the plants are full grown in July. As with real spinach, pick or cut stems close to the ground. If, because there are more exciting vegetables available, you do not need spinach beet for a few weeks, it is better to continue picking rather than let some leaves get old, which slows down production of tastier new growth. You can freeze any surplus for winter use or share with less fortunate neighbours. Growth is very slow in winter but you should have one or two pickings of young leaves from the row. In spring new growth starts, which can be used before the plants run to seed. Then dig them up for the compost heap and sow a fresh batch of seed in another part of the garden. The leaves of spinach beet are more fleshy than those of the true sorts of spinach and do not 'cook down' to very small quantities as does real spinach. Also, because spinach beet lacks the rather bitter taste of true spinach, children prefer it.

New Zealand Spinach (again not a true spinach or well known although most seedsmen offer seeds) is a summer/early autumn vegetable able to stand up to dry summer weather far better than ordinary summer spinach. This half-hardy vegetable is best given an early start by being sown in small pots in an unheated greenhouse or garden frame during mid to late April or during the first week of May. Set out plants during early June 60 cm (2 ft) apart. Leave at least 1 m (3 ft) between rows because the plants ramble over the ground. In southern England seeds can be sown in the open garden during the last fortnight of May. Sow two or three seeds where the plants are to grow and thin the seedlings to leave one at each station (the spot where each plant grows). Use a hoe to rid the ground of weeds when the plants are small; later, hand weed among the trailing spinach. Any extra long leading shoots may be nipped back to prevent the plants from becoming a nuisance to other vegetables growing nearby. Start picking by about mid July and continue picking fairly regularly till autumn. This spinach is an excellent cropper and it is worth while harvesting surplus tender shoots and leaves for the freezer.

Squash (see Vegetable Marrow, Squash and Pumpkin, p. 124)

Swede

Swedes, a variety of turnips developed, as the name suggests, by the Swedes, are hardier than turnips, longer-growing and do not become 'woody' as turnips do if not used when young. The gardener considers the turnip as a summer vegetable and the swede for winter use. If you live in the north sow swedes in early May; southern gardeners need not sow until later in May or in early June. 'Purple Top' is a popular variety. The swede is a member of the brassica (cabbage) family, although often considered more as a root crop and this means that it may suffer from Club Root infection (see p. 46). A new swede, Chignecto, has been specially bred for its resistance to this very nasty disease. Sow swede seeds in 2·5-cm (1-in) deep seed drills spaced 35 cm (15 ins) apart. Always fill the drills with water if the soil is dry and sow fairly thinly when the water has drained in. Thin the seedlings to 30 cm (12 ins) apart. Always keep well watered to prevent Turnip Flea Beetle damage (see p. 123). Swedes are usually left in the garden and dug when wanted in winter. They can, however, be stored (after cutting back any top growth to within 2·5 cm (1 in) of the swedes) in boxes of moist soil, sand or peat in the garden shed or an outhouse. Even in the coldest parts of the country it is not really worth storing swedes until Christmas.

Sweet corn

Also known as corn on the cob, it is not really a vegetable but a cereal and a form of maize. Varieties which can be relied upon to crop in any sort of summer in southern England are Northern Belle, First of All and Kelvedon Glory. Northern gardeners should, I think, try First of All or Northern Belle. I invariably give corn plants an early start by sowing two or three seeds in 9-cm (3½-in) Jiffy peat pots during late April or early May and house them in my unheated greenhouse or in a cold frame. Keep the pots fairly moist and thin the weaker seedlings to leave just one in each pot. When thinning corn seedlings just pinch off at the base of the seedlings otherwise you will disturb the roots of the remaining seedlings and corn plants hate any root disturbance. I harden off (see p. 58) the plants before setting them out in the garden during early June. Corn plants have several important requirements – light, warmth, lots of good food, plenty of water and block planting. Block planting means that instead of being in widely-spaced straight rows plants are grown in groups, which may be several short rows with the plants spaced about 30 cm (1 ft) apart or a cluster of four or five plants about 25 cm (9 ins) apart. I prefer the cluster way of corn growing in any suitable vacant spot. The plants need to be close so that sufficient ripe male pollen blows down from the male tassels at the top of the plants and on to the sticky female silks hanging from the embryo cobs, thus avoiding a poor set of grains on the cobs. Hand weed in between the plants. After fertilization the silks on the cobs change gradually from yellow-green to brown-black and also shrivel. Cobs should be ready for harvesting when the final shrivelled, brown-black stage is reached. I find, however, that it is always best to check on the condition of the grains before twisting off a cob by tearing back a part of the green sheath and pressing my thumbnail into a grain. If a watery fluid runs out, the cob is not ready and I replace the sheath and wait for a week before checking again. If the grain exudes a creamy liquor, all is well and the cob may be harvested. Do not leave cobs to age; aged cobs have grains full of tasteless, starchy paste. Cobs for home-freezing should always be blanched immediately after harvesting. Do not expect any specific pests in corn growing, but slugs will devour your corn seedlings so take precautions (see Chapter 2).

Sweet Peppers (see Capsicum, p. 54)

Swiss Chard (see Seakale Beet, p. 104)

Thyme (see Herbs, p. 74)

Tomatoes

Apples of Love was the name the first English tomato growers called this vegetable (actually a fruit used as a vegetable). To eat Apples of Love was thought to be 'naughty and corrupt', as John Gerard put it in 1597. However, tomatoes looked rather attractive in the flower garden and by 1805 the risk of being naughty and corrupt appeared to be worth taking. In that year John Abercrombie mentioned in his *Gardener's Calendar*: 'The fruits of these plants are, in some families, much used in soups and are also often used to pickle, both when young and green, and when at full growth and ripe maturity.' But tomatoes did not become fashionable until late in the last century, when there appears to have been a sort of tomato boom. My grandpa decided that tomato growing and brickmaking could go hand in hand and his brick and glass greenhouses were a sort of local wonder in north-west Kent. He very wisely built greenhouses sufficiently large for horses and carts to move through them, allowing for easy manuring and harvesting. Until the Second World War the tomato was considered far too tender to be grown outdoors in Britain. We now know differently and in southern England it is rare to come across a kitchen garden or an allotment without its row of tomato plants in summer.

Not all tomatoes are red; there are yellow tomatoes or red tomatoes faintly striped yellow. British gardeners did not take to white tomatoes when seeds were available; they lacked juice and didn't look tasty. Most tomato varieties are standard plants (plants to be trained as single stems); some varieties have a dwarf bush habit. Always choose standard sort for greenhouse-growing; standards or bush are suitable for the open garden or frame or cloche work. If you do not already have a special favourite among the many tomato varieties now on offer, there is a short list of recommended tomatoes on pp. 116–17. Some gardeners think tomato growing is difficult; others think raising plants is beyond their capabilities. True, the tomato is a half-hardy plant, but so is its close relative, the potato, and no gardeners consider potato growing difficult. When I was employed answering readers' enquiries for a gardening magazine, most of the queries involved tomato growing and many of the writers were obviously treating tomato plants as if they were jungle orchids. Hot, stuffy atmospheric conditions in a greenhouse lead to sick tomato plants and precious little in the way of a crop. I think it worth noting here that I did not receive one query about the health of outdoor tomato plants.

To raise plants in the orthodox manner presupposes that you have a greenhouse; a temperature of 18–21°C (65–70°F) by day, falling to about 16°C (60°F), must be maintained for good, even germination to take place. To reduce your heating costs you can curtain off a part of the greenhouse (using a large sheet of clear polythene film) and heat only this small area. Sowing time depends, too, on heating. When fuel was cheap gardeners thought late February was the right time to sow tomatoes for greenhouse plants. This meant first ripe tomatoes towards the end of June. Now, because it is far easier to keep the greenhouse (or a part of it) warm in March and April than in February, many tomato growers wait until late March before sowing seeds. Where plants are to be raised in a greenhouse and then moved to the open garden, always delay sowing until late March. The greenhouse-grown plants will start to have ripe tomatoes in July; the open garden (or cloched) plants start cropping in late July or in August, depending on the summer.

You will need a seed tray – and modern plastic trays are more easily kept clean than the traditional wood trays. You will also need a propagating compost, such as Levington Seed Compost. Fill the seed tray with the compost and compress it lightly with a block of wood or the palm of your hand. Sow about 50 tomato seeds evenly with each at about 2·5 cm (1 in) from its neighbour. Some tomato seeds are now sold in pelleted form and are more easily handled when sowing. Spread or sieve more compost over the seeds so that they are covered by about 1 cm ($\frac{1}{4}$ in). Water thoroughly with water at the same temperature as that of the greenhouse through a very fine rose on the watering-can. Place a sheet of glass over the tray and lay a sheet of brown paper on top of it. Turn the sheet of glass once each day to rid the underside of condensation. As soon as you see the small shoots of the germinating tomato seeds, remove the paper and glass. Make sure that the seedlings receive lots of light so that they are not 'drawn' (causing seedlings to become tall and spindly). Try to maintain a greenhouse temperature of 16–18°C (60–65°F) by day with a drop of a few degrees at night and in very dull weather. In very sunny weather greenhouse temperatures will soar during the day and ventilation may be necessary. You do not want your tomato seedlings to be cooked! How often you water is something you just have to learn by practice. The compost should be moist at all times – never dry and never soaking wet. Transfer the seedlings to pots when they have made one or two true leaves, i.e. typical tomato plant leaves. These may be 9-cm (3$\frac{1}{2}$-in) clay, plastic, whalehide or peat, and you need one pot for each seedling. A suitable compost is also needed and I suggest Levington Potting. Put some compost in each pot. Now dig the seedlings out of the tray. Hold them by one of the two seed leaves and never by a true leaf or by the stem. Plant the seedlings carefully and firmly in the pots, adding more compost and firming well. After the potting of the seedlings water well and stand them closely together on the greenhouse staging. To assist the seedlings to get over any shock received by the transplanting operation, raise temperatures to 21°C (70°F) by day dropping to 18°C (65°F) at night until you observe that the seedlings are growing on well. Keep the compost in the pots reasonably moist. Give ventilation in sunny weather and stand the pots apart as the seedlings grow so that they are not 'drawn'.

The plants will be ready for setting out in the greenhouse borders during May when they are about 20 cm (8 ins) tall with four or five large leaves. The soil in the borders should have been dug over in the previous autumn and well-rotted farmyard manure or garden compost incorporated into the top spit (depth of a spade or fork). Alternatively, the garden compost may have been spread as a mulch on the dug soil. If tomatoes have been grown in the borders for three seasons running, the soil (to a depth of about 30 cm or 1 ft) should be exchanged with good top soil from the garden and soaked well with water. Remove plants raised in clay, plastic, polythene or whalehide pots from the pots before planting. If you have plants in peat pots, tear away any parts of the pot which are dry. Take out planting holes 45 cm (18 ins) apart, fill with water and when it has soaked in, plant firmly but not deeply. Supports such as long bamboo canes should be pushed in the ground alongside each plant. There is usually sufficient sun heat in May to keep temperatures at a minimum of 18°C (65°F) by day but heat at night may be necessary to keep temperatures from falling below 10°C (50°F).

My own method of tomato propagation means that the first ripe tomatoes are not ready until at least a fortnight later but I have no worries as regards temperatures, relying exclusively on trapped sun heat in the greenhouse. I raise my tomato seedlings in the greenhouse these days simply because I now have a greenhouse. In the fifties, when I was raising tomato plants and tomatoes for sale, they were propagated in unheated garden frames. If you live in the south of England you can raise your own tomato plants and have excellent crops of tomatoes without investing first in a greenhouse.

However, to return to tomato sowing. During the last week of March or the first week of April, fork over a small part of one of the two greenhouse borders, remove any weeds and debris, firm gently and then rake level. A 2·5-cm (1-in) thick mulch of Levington Potting Compost is then spread over the dug soil. This mulch is firmed gently, too. An onion hoe is used to make 2·5-cm (1-in) deep seed drills spaced at 20 cm (8 ins) apart. Fill the drills with water, allow to drain away and sprinkle tomato seeds quite thickly. Fill the drills with the compost and firm by patting with the palm of the hand. Water occasionally (with a fine rose on the can) so that the seed bed does not get dry. When the seedlings have two or three seed leaves they are potted on into 9-cm (3½-in) Jiffies (peat pots) filled with Levington Potting Compost and stood closely together in shallow trenches made with an onion hoe in the greenhouse border. Attend to watering and ventilation and space

out the plants when they need more room. Plants can be set out in the greenhouse borders in late May or hardened off (see p. 58) before being set out in the open garden during the first half of June. Whether tomato plants were raised with or without heat, you simply must harden them off before planting them out in the garden.

Greenhouse cultivation

Let us return now to the plants set out in the greenhouse borders during May. Good ventilation is so important: not only should the greenhouse lights be fully open during most days but quite often the greenhouse door should be open too. If you have some form of heating in the greenhouse, keep night temperatures from falling below 10°C (50°F). Water regularly to keep the plants moist and to provide extra humidity which assists fertilization of the flowers and leads to a good set of fruitlets. Tie the plants loosely to the supports as they grow and pinch out all sideshoots in the leaf axils when the shoots are small. The removal of large shoots can lead to fungal Grey Mould disease. If the greenhouse border soil is not very fertile, feed the plants with home-made liquid manure (see p. 66) or with a proprietary tomato (preferably liquid) fertilizer, following the manufacturer's instructions. Start feeding when the first fruitlets develop on the first truss (the bottom cluster of fruitlets). In very hot weather and when trusses higher up are in flower, it may help in the fertilization of the flowers if you increase humidity in the greenhouse by spraying the plants with clean cold water. This must be done sufficiently early in the day so that when you close the door and the ventilators in the late evening the plants are quite dry. When the plants reach full height, pinch out the growing point at the top of each plant and make the final tie to the supports. Start harvesting your tomatoes when they are well coloured and fully ripe but not soft. Continue picking every few days. Pick all fruits as soon as they are ripe, otherwise they will soften; they may also split and be infected by fungal moulds. There are always neighbours, friends and relatives eager to share your bounty if you have surpluses. You can purée the surplus and freeze it or make red tomato chutney. Pick your last ripe tomatoes in late September or in early October. A few may still be green. Because autumn is the season of the fungi, I consider it better to clear the greenhouse of tomato plants before fungal growths appear on them. Any large green tomatoes will ripen off quite rapidly in a warm room; any small tomatoes are excellent for chutney making. After untying the plants, barrow them off to the compost heap. Dig the green-

house borders, flood them with water and spread on a thick mulch of garden compost in preparation for an equally good harvest next summer.

Outdoor cultivation

Hardened off standard tomato plants may be set out in the garden as soon as the danger of spring frosts is over. You can, of course, give cloche or frame protection to the plants to prevent frost damage. Plant them 45 cm (18 ins) apart with 75 cm (30 ins) between rows. Choose as sunny a position as possible in front of a south-facing wall if you have one. The planting operation is described on p. 111 but there may be no need to fill the planting holes with water if the soil is quite moist. Use 1·5-m (5-ft) bamboo canes or a simple trellis for support either immediately or when the frame lights or the cloches are removed. The plants will need regular, fairly copious waterings when they are growing well and when swelling fruits. As they grow tie them to the supports loosely to avoid cutting into the stems. Pinch out side shoots as on greenhouse plants (see p. 113) and the growing points of the plants at the second leaf above the last truss of small fruitlets or flowers in late July or early August. This top truss may never supply you with ripe tomatoes; it will, however, lead to small green tomatoes for green tomato chutney. Liquid feeds may be given (see p. 66) if considered necessary.

The first ripe tomatoes will be ready for picking in late July or in August, depending on the summer weather. In a cool summer the whole crop may not have ripened by mid September; by defoliating (stripping all leaves from plants), untying the plants from the supports, lowering them on to clean, dry straw spread over the ground, and setting cloches or frames in position, you can pick ripe tomatoes until late in October. Alternatively, during the last two weeks of September pick off every tomato from the plants. Sort the tomatoes into three groupings: (1) those red or pink and almost ready for use, (2) large green tomatoes and (3) small green fruits. Pile the red and pink tomatoes into dishes to be eaten within a fortnight. Store the large green fruits in a drawer or in Dutch trays indoors to ripen gradually throughout October. The small hard green tomatoes can be converted into chutney.

Bush tomatoes

The advantage of growing bush tomatoes is that they need almost no cultivation at all. No supports are necessary and there is no pinching out of sideshoots or 'stopping' of the plants in late July or early August. The disadvantages are that in a wet season slugs may devour a large proportion of the crop; it may also fall victim to soil organisms or to various fungal rots. Plant spacings vary depending on whether you are growing a rambling sort like the Amateur which needs at least 60 sq cm (2 sq ft) of surface space or a compact sort like Tiny Tim, needing only 30 sq cm (1 sq ft) of ground. Remember, too, that you have to walk round or among them to cultivate and harvest. Keep down weeds and when the plants topple on to the soil, spread clean, dry straw beneath the branches. If slugs are a problem, place slug destroyer beneath the straw. In a dry season pour water, and tomato feeds if you use them, through the straw now and then. Harvest tomatoes as they ripen and follow the ripening off process suggested for standard-type plants if there are unripe tomatoes in late September.

Tomato varieties

There are many and seedsmen give useful descriptions in their seed catalogues. Here are just a few good varieties you may care to try: *All are red unless other colours are mentioned.*

Ailsa Craig Uniform, medium sized, attractive tomatoes. An older variety noted for its good flavour.

Alicante Evenly-shaped, medium sized, good coloured tomatoes. Free from Greenback (see p. 122).

Big Boy An American salad tomato each weighing up to 500 gr (1 lb). Very good flavour.

Craigella Resembles 'Ailsa Craig' but free from Greenback (see p. 122).

Eurocross BB Medium sized, handsome and of good flavour. Free from Greenback and plants are resistant to one race of *Cladosporium* (see p. 121).

Gardener's Delight Long clusters of bright red, small tomatoes of excellent flavour. Recommended for outdoor growing.

Golden Amateur Golden-fruited counterpart of the better-known red variety 'The Amateur'. Dwarf bush for open garden, cloches or frames only.

Golden Sunrise Best-known yellow tomato. Tomatoes are medium size and bright yellow when ripe. Sweet and less acidic than the reds.

Histon Cropper Compact plants. Tomatoes are small to medium. An early ripener and recommended for frames, cloches and the open garden. Plants show resistance to Blight (see p. 120).

Marmande Typical continental salad type tomato. Flattish, round, few seeds, dull red skin. Average weight per tomato is about 125 gr (5 oz).

Moneymaker Best known and very widely grown tomato. Fruits are medium sized, handsome. Greenback-free.

Outdoor Girl Early ripening and for cloches, frames and open garden growing only. Tomatoes are dull red, somewhat small and sometimes of poor shape. The bottom truss may consist of forty tomatoes. Not the best tomato for flavour but generally liked.

Pixie A new bush tomato especially recommended for growing in pots and window-boxes. The fruit is small but flavour is good.

Roma Compact bush type tomato with typical Italian plum-shaped fruits. For open garden, cloches and frames only.

San Marzano Standard plant bearing typical Italian plum tomatoes. Not early ripening and best grown in a greenhouse.

Supercross Uniform, handsome, medium sized tomatoes of excellent flavour. Plants are immune to all strains of *Cladosporium* (see p. 121) and are unlikely to suffer from Tomato Mosaic virus. Greenback-free.

The Amateur Best known self-stopping bush tomato. Heavy cropper. Tomatoes are medium sized. Not recommended for greenhouse growing.

Tigerella Medium sized tomatoes which, when ripe, are red with faint gold stripes. Early ripening and Greenback-free.

Tiny Tim Miniature bush. Small tomatoes are bright red, of good flavour and with few seeds. Not recommended for greenhouse growing.

Yellow Perfection Yellow and similar to Golden Sunrise.

Buying tomato plants

There is little choice of variety and Moneymaker is the tomato most usually offered for sale. Choose sturdy, deep green plants with (where possible) the first flower truss just opening its buds. Many tomato plants on sale in late spring have not been hardened off and if you intend planting bought plants outdoors without frame or cloche protection, it pays to harden off the plants (see p. 58). If you have no greenhouse, small frame or cloches, just take the plants under cover at night.

Other ways of growing tomatoes

Elsewhere you may come across references to Ring Culture. This method was a boon to the commercial grower with a greenhouse soil quite incapable of producing a good crop of tomatoes. I have never wished to complicate growing any food crop so I have not tried Ring Cultivation and do not recommend it to you.

If you have soil troubles there is now a far easier way of dispensing with the soil. I am thinking of the polythene bag method – Tom Bags, Gro Bags – which suit standard or bush tomatoes; they are filled with a suitable compost in which two or three tomato plants can be grown. Not only are these bags of use to the gardener with poor greenhouse soil but they are of immense value in a yard, a patio or on a town balcony. Instructions are provided with each bag. In brief, cultivation consists of watering and giving an occasional liquid feed. Fix the supports alongside the bags, taking care not to puncture them. The compost may subsequently be used for spring flowering bulbs – hyacinths, tulips, daffodils.

Tomatoes are naturals for tubs and pots or disused polythene buckets, provided you make a few holes in the base so that good drainage is provided. A 25-cm (10-in) pot will take one standard plant, a 30-cm (12-in) pot two and a 35-cm (14-in) pot three. Bush-type tomatoes also do well in pots and Tiny Tim is worth growing even in a window-box. I suggest you use a lightweight, soil-less compost like Levington Potting. Cultivate as for outdoor-grown plants.

Although it is more usual to remove protection from plants in the garden as soon as standard sorts need more headroom, it is possible to keep the plants protected so that fruiting starts earlier. You may either set out the plants in 15-cm (6-in) deep trenches and behead the plants when they reach the 'roof',

obtaining two or three trusses on standard-type plants. With bush sorts in frames or beneath cloches you have no worries about headroom but pay particular care to control slugs which make a beeline for the comfortable living quarters of well-watered frames and cloched rows in summer, particularly where bush plants are mulched with straw to keep the fruits from being mud-splashed or attacked by soil organisms.

Tomato troubles

Some of the pests and diseases which affect the tomato are listed below. Where possible precautionary measures are suggested.

Blight A fungus disease. Rare on greenhouse plants but can be a nuisance on outdoor-grown plants in a warm, wet autumn. Dark brown to black streaks show on leaves and stems. The small brown markings on the fruits enlarge and rotting starts. If you live where blight is a normal hazard I suggest you try Histon Cropper. Unwins of Histon claim that this tomato is highly resistant to blight. During the 1950s my crop of Moneymaker tomatoes once suffered badly, and I now usually grow Outdoor Girl and Supercross in the garden. Blight can be a great nuisance on green tomatoes stored indoors to ripen off; you may notice no symptoms on the plants nor when picking the tomatoes. Keep the fruits away from each other so that Blight spores do not pass from fruit to fruit. Papier mâché egg cartons and trays are useful storage containers. Ask at supermarkets for the larger egg trays.

Root diseases Common when tomatoes are grown in badly drained soil. Plants wilt and die. Always grow tomatoes in well-drained soil or containers.

Stem Rot A rare but nasty disease causing plants to wilt, rot and die. A soft brown/black canker shows low down on the main stem; a similar infection may appear higher on the stem. Pull up and burn infected plants. The soil in the greenhouse borders must be replaced and the interior of the greenhouse cleaned with disinfectant. The disease may be imported, so, when possible, grow your own tomato plants from seed obtained from a reputable seedsman.

Damping off Stems of small seedlings shrivel, topple over and die. This disease is caused by several different soil fungi. Cheshunt Compound may halt an attack but does not cure affected seedlings. Prevent the disease by using clean seed boxes, clean water. Never use garden top soil for propagation of seeds. I have never had this trouble when using sifted garden compost in seed trays and pots or Levington Composts.

Grey Mould A grey powdery fungus appears on stems, foliage and fruits of greenhouse-grown plants, usually in early autumn; seldom earlier in the season. Affected parts rot. Can occur in summer if ventilation is poor or if large wounds are left when side growths are pinched out. Always remove side shoots when small and give greenhouse plants plenty of ventilation. Always water protected tomato plants during the day and not of an evening. Clear the greenhouse of tomato plants in September before this common disease puts in an appearance.

Tomato Leaf Mould Caused by three strains of the fungus *Cladosporium fulvum*. A very common disease of greenhouse tomatoes. I have not seen this disease but am told yellowish spots appear on the upper surfaces of the leaves and a pale greyish mould on the underside. Mild attacks may be controlled by proprietary sprays based on manganese and zinc. If left, the disease (which appears in June and July) leads to sick plants and poor crops. Adequate ventilation prevents the disease and there are also tomato varieties which are immune to one or more strains of *Cladosporium*.

Blossom End Rot A brown or black circular patch forms at the blossom end (the bottom end) of the fruit and rotting commences. There is no cure. May be due to over-watering, irregular watering or to the use of feeds containing excessive nitrogen.

Blotchy Ripening A very common disorder. Tomatoes have irregular, unripe, yellow patches on red fruit. Unbalanced fertilizer feeds are suspected of causing this trouble, as are high greenhouse atmospheric temperatures accompanied by low soil temperatures. The tomatoes usually ripen completely if picked and stored in a warm room for a few days.

Dry Set Fruitlets set but they do not swell and remain pinhead sized. A common disorder where humidity is low in the greenhouse at flowering time.

Flowers Drop There may be other causes but this rather common disorder is usually blamed on the plants being short of water at the roots.

Fruits Split Another common trouble, usually only of greenhouse tomatoes, although splitting can occur on outdoor-grown plants in a dry summer. It is due to a lack of water in the soil followed by a heavy watering – in the case of outdoor-grown plants this means heavy rain. Always make sure that your tomato plants are kept well supplied with water at their roots.

Greenback The stalk end (the back end) of ripe tomatoes stays green or is yellow. Said to be caused by unbalanced chemical feeds but more likely due to strong sunlight. Never remove healthy leaves from tomato plants. Shade the greenhouse, frames or cloches if you consider that far too much bright sunlight may harm your tomatoes. Some new varieties are offered as 'Greenback-free'.

Greenhouse Whitefly Small winged insects suck sap from plants. When disturbed they flutter around like tiny moths. Spraying with derris is helpful. After the greenhouse has been cleared of all plants, fumigate with a smoke generator.

Red Spider Mite Very small mites make a web over the leaf surfaces and may be observed through a lens. Their action weakens plants. Prevent by keeping the greenhouse atmosphere reasonably humid; the mites like a dry atmosphere. Spray affected plants with derris on several occasions. In late autumn after the greenhouse has been cleared of plants use a smoke generator to fumigate.

Slugs Watch out for slug damage to tomato seedlings. I hunt for slugs in the evening, using a torch. In a wet season slugs can devour a large part of the crop on bush plants, and can also be a nuisance on ripening tomatoes on standard plants. In a wet season it pays to remove mulches around garden-grown standard tomato plants during late August. Transfer the mulching material to the compost heap and search for any slugs and kill them. My pool fish eat crushed slug with gusto!

Turnip

Although gardening books occasionally mention winter turnips, these are now rarely grown by gardeners; instead the swede is grown because of its hardiness and its milder, sweeter flavour. The gardener now concentrates on the quick-growing summer sorts of turnip. Popular varieties are Golden Ball, Golden Perfection, Milan White, Purple Top Milan. The flesh colour can be white or yellow. For success with turnips, rapid plant growth must be fostered. This means that temperatures must be suitable and the soil must hold moisture in dry weather, so delay sowing until the soil is warming up in April. Sowings may be made on and off until mid July. The June and July sowings must be made in wet seed drills and the seedlings and growing plants watered often unless the summer is abnormally wet. I for one have no great need of turnips when peas and beans are pickable and leave turnip sowing until a piece of ground falls vacant in late June or early July. The turnips are ready in September when a few are used in stews and casseroles and the bulk are then pulled for freezer storage.

When sowing turnips make seed drills at no deeper than 2·5 cm (1 in) and leave 30 cm (12 ins) between rows. Thin the seedlings to 10–15 cm (4–6 ins) apart when they are small. Keep the plants free from weeds and well supplied with water for necessary quick growth.

The Turnip Flea Beetle, which makes lots of tiny holes in the leaves of turnip seedlings (and in the seedlings of other brassicas – yes, the turnip belongs to the cabbage family but is classed as a root vegetable), should not be among your gardening worries. This pest likes dry conditions so keep turnip and brassica seedlings well watered in dry weather. However, if things should go wrong you can dust the seedlings with derris.

Club Root (see p. 46) can attack turnips. Follow the preventive measures outlined on pp. 46–8.

Another possible pest is the Turnip Gall Weevil (see p. 48) but I have never come across a turnip suffering from this trouble. If it occurs, your turnips will most certainly look disfigured, but the damage is only surface-deep and the galls can be easily removed when the turnips are being peeled for use or for blanching.

The turnip is one of the few eat-all vegetables. Although we usually grow turnips for their swollen roots, the foliage is a pseudo-spinach. For those who like turnip tops I suggest the sowing of Imperial Green Globe (syn. Greentop White) in August or early in September. Do not thin the seedlings and harvest leaves as for spinach (see p. 105) in winter and spring.

Vegetable marrow, squash and pumpkins (including courgettes)

Understanding what a marrow is, what a squash is, how pumpkins fit in to the picture and when a squash or a marrow is a courgette, can send the new gardener or plot-holder round the twist. In American English any sort of vegetable marrow is a squash, but we have not adopted the word. Until some time in the nineteenth century we arbitrarily split these edible gourds into two divisions, Gourds and Pompions (or pumpkins). All-green and green with striped longish gourds gained in popularity, and some wag (probably a seedsman) compared the flesh to the marrow in a marrowbone – hence 'marrow' – and another wag added the prefix 'vegetable'. But other squashes continued to be grown. Where a name was wanted for a special squash, somebody was always ready to supply one, so we have the South African Marrow, the Argentine Marrow. The attractive Patty Pan squashes of the American garden have been renamed for British gardeners – Custard White and Custard Yellow. The pumpkin, a close relative, has resisted changes to its mame. The Courgette is something quite new to British gardeners. In France and Italy vegetable marrows are never permitted to swell to the size they usually become in the British garden and are invariably cut when about 10 cm (4 ins) long. The French are renowned for their practical approach to any subject and in gardening they make no exception. To them, a marrow is a gourd (Courge) and cut when small, they are simply small gourds (Courgettes). In recent years we have come to like courgettes; they are simply small marrows. I am sorry to have gone to such lengths to explain all of this but I am very aware of how even seasoned gardeners shy away from growing squashes and courgettes because the names put them off.

Let us now deal with the popular vegetable marrow which may be considered here as our standard 'squash' against which we can compare the cultivation of all other edible gourds.

Because the vegetable marrow is a half-hardy subject liable to a quick death if touched by a late spring frost, it is most unwise to sow seeds in the open garden before mid to late May. Of course, protection can be afforded. Seeds may be sown under cloches or in frames or jam jars (open end downwards) set over the stations. There are two sorts of plants. Most of the reasonably compact bush varieties need 1 sq m (1 sq yd) of surface area. I find you can get two plants in the same area if you sow (or set out plants) in the American way by having two plants spaced at about 15 cm (6 in) apart. The trailing varieties of marrow take up much more space and are not suited to frame growing; they are ideal camouflage plants if you wish to hide a compost heap, a pile of autumn leaves or the weedy garden next door. Set the plants at the base of the heaps and encourage the main stems of the plants to travel upwards. To hide your neighbour's weedy garden or to lose the view of the local gas works all summer long, you need a strong trellis. If the garden fence is a wire mesh affair, you have half of your trellis to hand. Simply heighten the fence, using a few posts or poles and several strands of wire. Alternatively increase the height with wire or plastic garden mesh fixed to 1·8-m (6-ft) posts. Set out plants or sow seeds 30 cm (12 in) apart alongside the trellis. Trailing marrows can also be grown on tepees. These are four long bamboo canes tied together at the apex and with soft wire or string wound round the canes, giving an openwork wigwam effect. There is no need to confine marrow growing simply to your kitchen garden, as the giant gold bell flowers, the large leaves and swelling marrows are an attractive sight on a tepee. The marrow is a greedy, thirsty plant. You need good rich soil and plenty of water in dry summer weather to avoid having disappointing marrows. They can be started early by sowing with protection (greenhouse, frame or cloche) in late April or early May. Follow the same procedure as for cucumber propagation (see p. 64). Always harden off (see p. 58) plants in late May or early June if they are to go out in the garden. Neither bush nor trailing sorts need any pruning but I suggest that you pinch out the growing point of the main stem of trailing marrows grown on tall supports, just as with cucumbers (see p. 67).

All gourd plants bear two different kinds of flowers; ripe

pollen from the male flowers has to reach and fertilize the female blooms which have embryo marrows tucked behind them. When the first female blooms open in July, gardeners often take a hand in the fertilization process, because each flower remains in pristine condition for only a few hours before noon and bees and other insects may miss the occasional marrow flower, or the marrow plants in one's own garden may be bearing only female flowers. To hand-pollinate, pick a freshly opened male, strip off the petals and gently rub its single central 'core' into the divided centre of a female. Marrow plants should be well watered; sink a flowerpot alongside each plant and water and any liquid feeds are then applied via the pots. Mulching marrow plants with straw also helps keep the soil around them moist. If you fear slug damage to the swelling marrows, raise them on to pieces of slate or tile, which are seldom crossed by marauding slugs. The vegetable marrow is a summer vegetable and one which is very much a come-and-cut-and-come again crop. Never leave marrows to get super-sized, woody and lacking the little flavour any marrow can boast. No marrow is fit for eating if you can't pierce the skin easily with your thumbnail. Some folk allow a marrow to ripen on the plant either for jam-making – and there really is no jam to compare with marrow and ginger – or to have garden-grown marrow at Christmas. Where a marrow is left on the plant, that plant then ceases to set more young marrows. I tried storing a marrow myself on one occasion and must confess I found it as unpleasant after cooking as I had anticipated it would be. But perhaps I am too choosey. Quite a number of gardeners really enjoy stored marrow at Christmas. I hope the habit does not put their kids off marrow for life! Your marrow plants will keep in regular production from late July until late September with perhaps a marrow or two in October if the autumn weather is kind.

Grow summer squashes in exactly the same way as ordinary vegetable marrow. In the list on pp. 128–9 you will see that I have divided squashes into two groups – summer and winter. Winter squashes are not harvested until they are fully ripe and with solid, woody skins. Plants bear two or three fruits only. Cut them from the plants in late September or early October. Store winter squashes in a cool but frostproof place. If you can hang squashes in mesh net bags (one squash per bag) from the ceiling, so much the better. They keep well until Christmas; sometimes until February.

The pumpkin is sown, grown and harvested in exactly the same way as winter squashes. Because pumpkins are the heavyweights of the garden, plants are best left to trail over the ground or over heaps of garden compost or autumn leaves rather than be trained on a fence or trellis. Store them singly on a shelf in a cool, frost-proof place. But does anybody in the family know how to cook winter squash or pumpkin? Our American friends rave over both of them but go to a lot of trouble preparing squash or pumpkin with fruits and cream. When I grew winter squashes I tried cooking them like vegetable marrow and did not like them at all. German cooks add pumpkin to soups. When I grew pumpkins I candied a part of one gigantic gourd and found that candied pumpkin really is something for the children.

And now a word about courgettes. Bush sorts of vegetable marrow are chosen for courgette production. Zucchini is a variety that comes to mind at once for dark-skinned courgettes; there is also the new Golden Zucchini with a bright yellow skin. Sow and grow courgette plants as ordinary bush-type vegetable marrow but cut the marrows when they are very small. The more frequently you harvest, the more courgettes you will go on harvesting.

All of these edible gourds would be so easy to grow were it not for a killer virus disease called *Cucumber Mosaic* – not the worry in cucumber cultivation that it so often is with vegetable marrow growing. The trouble shows in July, when the foliage becomes mottled with light yellow patches (do not confuse these with the grey patches on healthy leaves of 'Zucchini'). Plants are stunted and any marrows are small and malformed. There is no cure. Plants must be dug up and burnt. Several reasons were offered in the past for the origin of this killing virus and current thought places the blame on chickweed as the prime cause. Apparently much chickweed is already infected with the virus and aphids quickly transmit it to our marrow plants. It is impossible to prevent chickweed from germinating in fertile soil, so until a resistant-to-virus marrow is bred I am afraid we must sometimes expect to lose marrow plants. From my own observations it seems the earlier than usual plants are more likely to suffer. Next season I shall sow seeds outdoors in late May rather than getting the plants on early by sowing with protection in late April or early May. The virus is also more active in some areas than in others. You may never meet the trouble. It also seems to me that the pumpkin and winter squashes are almost never troubled by this virus disease. Among summer squashes, the Vegetable Spaghetti is less likely to be inconvenienced by the virus than other sorts.

Some varieties of squash and pumpkin

Variety	Season of use	Bush or trailer	Remarks
All Green Bush	summer	bush	Ordinary vegetable marrow
Custard White	summer	bush	Looks like a custard pie – but white
Custard Yellow	summer	bush	Looks just like a custard pie
Gold Nugget	summer or winter	bush	Like large green grapefruit in summer. Ripe squashes are gold
Golden Delicious	winter	trailer	Large and round or turban-shaped; gold skin
Golden Zucchini	summer	bush	Yellow-skinned courgettes
Hubbards Golden	winter	trailer	Rather like Golden Delicious and squashes weigh about 3 kg (6 lb) each
Hubbards Green	winter	trailer	The green-skinned form of Hubbards Golden. Probably most popular winter squash in the USA
Long Green Bush	summer	bush	Ordinary vegetable marrow

Variety	Season of use	Bush or trailer	Remarks
Long Green Trailing	summer	trailer	Ordinary vegetable marrow
Long White Bush	summer	bush	Ordinary vegetable marrow with white skin
Long White Trailing	summer	trailer	As above
Mammoth syn. King of the Mammoths	winter	trailer	Invariably chosen by gardeners who grow pumpkins
Sweet Dumpling	summer or winter	trailer	Small white-skinned and ideal for stuffing and serving individually
Table Dainty	summer	trailer	Like ordinary vegetable marrow but small. Ideal for exhibiting at local Shows
Tender and True	summer	bush but with trailing tendency	Round but flattened, green-skinned. Early cropper
Vegetable Spaghetti	summer or winter	trailer	Like Long Green. Trailing in appearance. The flesh is likened to spaghetti and may be eaten hot or cold
Zucchini	summer	bush	Like ordinary vegetable marrow. Popular for courgette production

4 Make room for some fruit, too

Apples

In Chapter 1 I have given some reasons why apples and other fruits (pears, plums, damsons) should not normally be planted on allotments. But every garden should, where possible, have a couple of fruit trees and the apple is a general favourite. You need an open, sunny site and a soil which drains well. On the other hand, the soil must not dry out rapidly in dry summer weather. I have explained in Chapter 1 how a light, sandy soil can be improved so that it holds water better, and it is a waste of time to plant in poor soil. If you have taken over a new garden with poor soil or soil which is infested with such horrors as bindweed and creeping thistle, grow vegetables for a year or two before planting fruit trees. Garden compost for vegetable growing will improve the soil and make it suitable for fruit trees. Apple trees may be planted at any time between November and March. November is preferable and orders for young trees should be placed well in advance and with a reputable nurseryman specializing in fruit. Plant apple trees away from the kitchen garden proper as they do not need regular feeds. Cooking apples are more tolerant of very fertile soil and if that's all you've got, I suggest that you stick to cookers. Although some apples give a good account of themselves crop-wise on their own, all varieties do better if a suitable pollinator is to hand. Most apples need just one cross-pollinator; a few need two (see p .137). To have a good set of fruit, the two or three trees must come into bloom at the same time so that bees and other insect pollinators will transfer ripe pollen from flower to flower. The large standard-type trees of old orchards are now not favoured as it is far easier to prune and harvest from bush trees. Apples and other tree fruits are grafted on to varying rootstocks. How a bush apple will flourish depends on the rootstock on which the nurseryman has grafted the varieties of apple you wish to grow. Here are the usual rootstocks for apples and something about them.

M VII Semi-dwarfing. The trees tend to build up branches for three or four years before cropping regularly and well. Needs good fertile soil. If suckers (unwanted growths from the rootstock) are made, these must be dug out from around the trees.

M IX Very dwarfing. Needs a soil of higher fertility than is usual for apples. Comes into bearing quickly. Trees need permanent stakes to support them.

M 26 Dwarfing but more vigorous than M IX and does not need the sort of fertile soil required by M IX rootstock. Trees usually need permanent stakes.

MM 106 Semi-dwarfing. Trees are usually smaller than those on rootstock M VII. Highly fertile soils are not needed.

M 11 and **MM 111** Vigorous. Usually chosen for garden bush trees. Trees often need more attention as regards pruning than bush apples on other rootstocks.

If you are not sure which rootstock fits in with your soil conditions, discuss the subject with the nurseryman. This brings us to another point. Unless you know about fruit tree training bush apples are about the easiest-shaped trees for amateurs to grow. By all means look at and admire well-trained cordons, espaliers and fans. There are a number of fine trees trained by these methods in the Garden of the Royal Horticultural Society at Wisley, Surrey, but they need regular pruning and some expertise as regards training in the building up of the permanent framework of the trees.

Let me assume that you have chosen the varieties of apple you want and on rootstocks suited to your soil. The trees are likely to arrive at a time when either the soil is too wet or you just haven't got time to plant them. Do not leave the trees in their wrappings. Unpack them and heel them in. Cover the roots with the excavated soil. The trees will remain in good condition for several weeks if this is necessary. When you can get down to planting them, use a garden fork to ease the roots out of the ground and, if they are dry, soak them in a tub of water for an hour or so. Planting distances depend on the rootstock and the following distances are recommended for bush apples:

Rootstock	Distance in metres (feet) between trees
Bush on vigorous stock	6 (20)
Semi-dwarf on moderately vigorous stock	3·5 (12)
Dwarf bush on weak-growing stock	2·7 (9)

Make the planting holes sufficiently large to fit the roots comfortably. Cut back any damaged or extra long roots. Correct depth of planting is important with fruit trees. Look for the soil mark (a change in the colour of the bark) low down on the trees to see where the underground part of the trees started before the nurseryman dug them up. Plant so that the soil mark is level with the surrounding soil. All fruit trees need supports at planting. These can be permanent where the rootstock is not vigorous, or temporary. Temporary supports are removed when the trees have taken hold and are growing well. Position strong stakes or poles before filling in the holes when the tree roots have been spread out in them. Using a shovel or a spade, gradually replace the earth. As you fill, tread firmly so that the roots are embedded into the soil. Immediately after planting, tie the trees to the supports with special tree ties so that no chafing of the bark occurs. Now spread garden compost or strawy manure around the newly-planted trees. If rabbits gnaw young trees where you live, fix metre-high small-mesh chicken wire around each tree and about 2·5 cm (1 in) from the bark.

Gardeners usually start off with two- or three-year-old trees already partly shaped by the nurseryman who supplied them. If the trees are on dwarfing stocks, they soon start to bear fruit. No pruning is usually needed when trees of this sort are planted apart from the cutting off of any twigs damaged during transit to your home. However, it is cheaper to buy maidens (one-year-old trees). With these trees the gardener has, however, to carry out the initial, formative pruning; they will also not come into bearing so quickly.

A one-year-old tree may have laterals (called 'feathers' by fruit growers) or consist of just a single stem with perhaps only a few weak side growths. Most gardeners want open-centred trees and they have this in mind when pruning their fruit trees. When

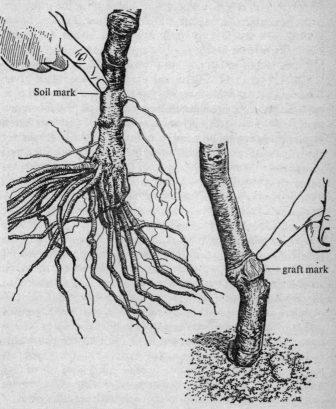

Soil mark

graft mark

starting the initial pruning of a maiden tree immediately after planting, the gardener inspects the tree. If the young tree has no 'feathers' and it has been grafted on dwarfing stock, the tree should be headed back (cut back) to leave it at 50–60 cm (20–24 ins) tall. Trees on very vigorous rootstocks are headed back to leave them at 67–75 cm (27–30 ins) tall. With 'feathered maidens' the initial pruning technique is different if the 'feathers' (lateral growths) are strong and not less than 45 cm (18 ins) above soil level. In such cases the tree may be headed back to the topmost strong lateral. Three or four suitably strong, well-spaced laterals are left and all others (including any lower down the trunk) are cut off cleanly with a pruning knife, sharp secateurs or flower scissors. The few laterals which have been left on the tree to eventually become its first few branches are then pruned back to half their length and to an outward-facing bud. In the following late autumn or early winter prune the laterals once again in the same way. Allow another year of growth and each tree will have made six or eight branches to be pruned back in late autumn again. Finally each tree will have a framework of twelve to sixteen permanent branches, all pointing outwards. During the summer always pinch off any new shoots (but not if they are bearing fruits) which tend to grow into the centre of the trees. If you aim at having open-centred trees, not only will the trees look neat but there will be adequate light and air circulation round the fruits. A trained orchardist knows at a glance when a tree needs further pruning. The amateur food grower is advised to keep any pruning of bush trees to a minimum. A branch which is too close to its neighbour or which gets in your way can, of course, be sawn off and the wound painted over with lead paint or a tree-sealing compound. Always remove large branches and sideshoots in winter when the tree is dormant (more or less inactive).

Where an established apple tree makes excessive side growths and little fruit, the gardener is usually to blame. The tree is over-nourished and has been planted in or too near the rich, fertile soil of the kitchen garden. Young apple trees benefit from regular, heavy waterings in a dry summer; established bush apples may benefit from water in a very dry summer, particularly if you live in the drier, eastern half of Britain. Apple trees are often grown in grass, but leave a circle of bare soil 60 cm (2 ft) in radius around each tree if you want to do this. Other garden plants can be grown between young apple trees but do not over-fertilize the soil with manure or garden compost. Peas, beans, root crops and annual flowers could be chosen. But do not try growing vegetables or flowers between established apple trees.

Apple trees sometimes benefit from an autumn-spread mulch of well rotted farmyard manure or garden compost; they will often crop well without any added plant foods. It is up to the gardener to decide if and when any additional nutrients may be needed by his apple trees.

In June do not be worried when you notice many fruitlets on the ground. This is the June Drop when apple trees regulate the crop to be matured that season. Some gardeners follow the June Drop by thinning more of the fruitlets to obtain fewer but larger apples. The king apple, the larger, sometimes misshapen fruitlet in the centre of a fruit cluster, is the first to be pinched off. During July a further thinning may be undertaken to leave each apple left on the trees plenty of space.

Apples are ready for picking when they part easily from the branch. To harvest an apple, grasp it and lift it upwards and give a slight twist. But just because an apple is ready for harvesting does not always mean that this is also the correct time to eat it or cook it. See the chart on p. 137. When picking apples handle them as if they are eggs, especially if the fruits are to be stored. Bruised apples rot quickly in store. Always harvest apples for storing on a dry day and store only unbruised and absolutely unblemished apples. If you wrap each apple in a perforated clear polythene bag you will be able to inspect the stored fruits easily and to avoid any fungal rot on one apple passing to the rest. Apples need a very cool, ventilated storage place. I suggest the garage as about the best place these days or a garden shed. Dutch trays (freely given by supermarkets and greengrocers) are excellent storage containers because they stack well.

After harvesting your last apples, collect any decaying apples from around the trees and put them inside the compost heap. After leaf fall, tidy around the trees. All leaves and other debris can go on the compost pile. If the soil has been compacted by feet during harvesting, fork it shallowly to loosen it. If the trees are in grass, mow for the last time this year and leave the mowings where they are. If your apple trees are not making the good growth apply a mulch of farmyard manure or garden compost.

Family trees

These deserve a mention, I think. Each tree is grafted with three different but compatible (pollen-wise for good fertilization) apple varieties. Examples are:

Red Ellison	Discovery	Grenadier
Cox's Orange Pippin	Egremont Russet	Worcester Pearmain
Laxton's Superb	Golden Delicious	Charles Ross

Plant Family Trees at 2·5 m (8 ft) apart. Do not prune excessively. Tip back any strong new growths in winter; cut back weak new growths to a strong bud so that better, stronger growth is promoted. Remove any strong growing vertical branches.

Apple troubles

The apple can suffer from at least fifty different diseases, disorders and pests. Several of the more common troubles are described here, with, where possible, suggested precautionary ways of preventing them.

Brown Rot Circular brown patches appear on fruits. Small white pustules form in rings on the affected patches. Fruits gradually rot and blacken. Caused by a fungus entering the fruit via a wound in the skin. Keep trees well watered when necessary in dry summer weather so that the skins do not split. See also Apple Sawfly and Codling Moth below. Bury all infected apples within the compost heap or in the ground. Branches and fruit spurs can be affected and should be cut off and burnt in early summer.

Canker Buds, spurs and branches die. Cox's Orange Pippin, James Grieve and Worcester Pearmain are frequently affected by this fungal disease. Always seal large pruning wounds to prevent entry of the fungus. Cut back affected branches to clean wood during late autumn or winter. Ancient apple trees in neglected gardens are usually sufferers from this disease. Grub up sick trees and burn them.

Some varieties of apples to choose

Name	Dessert or cooker	Flowering time	Pick	Use
Arthur Turner	C	MS	July–Sept.	July–Nov.
Beauty of Bath	D	E	Early Aug.	Aug.
Blenheim Orange*	D	MS	Oct.	Nov.–Jan.
Bramley's Seedling*	C	MS	Late Sept.	Nov.–Mar.
Charles Ross	D	MS	Oct.	Oct.–Nov.
Cox's Orange Pippin	D	MS	Oct.	Nov.–Jan.
Discovery	D	E	Aug.	Aug.
Early Victoria	C	MS	July–Sept.	July–Sept.
Egremont Russet	D	ES	Oct.	Oct.–Nov.
Ellison's Orange	D	MS	Sept.–Oct.	Sept.–Oct.
Fortune (Laxton's Fortune)	D	MS	Oct.	Oct.–Nov.
George Cave	C	E	Aug.–Sept.	Aug.–Sept.
Grenadier	C	MS	Aug.	Aug.
James Grieve	D	MS	Sept.–Oct.	Sept.–Oct.
Lane's Prince Albert	C	MS	Oct.	Nov.–Apr.
Laxton's Superb†	D	MS	Oct.	Nov.–Feb.
Lord Derby	C	L	Oct.	Nov.–Jan.
Lord Lambourne	D	E	Oct.	Oct.–Dec.
Merton Worcester	D	MS	Sept.–Oct.	Sept.–Oct.
Newton Wonder	C	L	Oct.	Oct.–Apr.
Spartan	D	MS	Oct.	Nov.–Jan.
Sunset	D	MS	Oct.	Oct.–Dec.
Worcester Pearmain	D	MS	Sept.–Oct.	Sept.–Oct.

* These need two different pollinators nearby. All of the other varieties listed above will crop better if another variety is near. Late flowering varieties are worth choosing if you fear a late spring frost may kill apple blossom in your garden.

† Do not rely on this apple as a pollinator; also has a habit of producing a good crop every second year.

Scab Black spot on fruit spreads to form a large blackened patch. Fruits may be misshapen. Leaves can be attacked and have brown, circular spots. The fungal spores over-winter on fallen leaves so always collect these and debris from around apple trees each autumn and add it all to the compost heap. Proprietary sprays are available and always follow the manufacturer's instructions closely. Never use any sprays based on mercurial compounds and do not spray when bees may be harmed.

Apple Sawfly Larvae of this fly feed on the swelling fruits and make ribbon-like scars on them. The damaged flesh has an unpleasant smell. A nice way of dealing with this pest is to pen some hens around the apple trees and leave the hens to scratch and unearth pupating larvae from the soil. A less pleasant way is to spray with nicotine twice: the first time when petals fall; the second a week later. If you use nicotine do bear in mind that it is poisonous.

Codling Moth Possibly the most common trouble of apples. Caterpillars tunnel into the fruits and feed on and around the cores. Fix sacking or corrugated cardboard below the main branches in mid July. The caterpillars will hibernate in cocoons beneath these materials. Remove the covers in December and, if you have hens, leave them to pick out the cocoons. Otherwise burn the covers.

Lackey Moth The small caterpillars weave tents and eat leaves of apples and other trees. They leave the tents when larger and continue eating foliage. Can be a serious nuisance on young or dwarfed trees. Look for tents in late spring and kill the caterpillars within.

Blackberry

An ideal, out of the way spot for blackberries would be on a wire-mesh garden fence. You can increase the height of a 1·2-m (4-ft) fence to about 1·8 m (6 ft) with the aid of a few strong posts and a couple of wires running horizontally. Alternatively, erect a simple trellis of stout posts linked together with wires in a sunny position. A trellis of this sort could be a 'divide' between the lawn and flower garden and the vegetable garden. Metal and plastic garden meshes are also ideal forms of support for trained brambles. If you are considering brambles on the garden fence choose sorts without prickles. If your garden is large, by all means choose fine prickly blackberries like Parsley Leaved and Bedford Giant, bearing in mind, though, that they need from 3–3·5 m (10–12 ft) of row space. Do not even consider Himalaya Giant – unless your intention is keep a herd of buffalo from entering your garden! I grew Merton Thornless for many years, but the main drawback with this is that when berries are being harvested they do not readily part company from the bush. In some seasons this blackberry does not make new strong canes for bearing the next summer's crop. Oregon Thornless is now the popular thornless blackberry. It cannot be expected to grow and crop well unless given first-class fertile soil. Smoothstem and Thornfree are two newer prickle-free blackberries.

Blackberries are excellent allotment fruits but some local authorities forbid plot-holders to plant them because old-type prickly sorts were commonly planted and then allowed to go on the rampage to the discomfort and annoyance of other plot-holders. So check up on your rent agreement before planting blackberries on your allotment. If you are allowed to grow this fruit, the surplus can be sold and bring in enough cash to cover all allotment expenses – seeds, plants, tubers, tools, etc. I know. Between 1955 and 1960 I sold 0·25 tonnes (¼ ton) of my own allotment grown blackberries as well as supplying a local garden shop with rooted runner blackberry plants. Training blackberries on the wire fences seemed a good idea and proved profitable.

Plant blackberries in late autumn. Take out holes large enough to take the straggly roots with ease. The 'soil mark' (see p. 132) indicates the correct depth of planting. Plant firmly but take care that any young buds are not damaged when doing this. Planting distances can be from 1·8–2·5 m (6–8 ft) between bushes. After planting prune back the canes (if the nurseryman has not done so) to leave them only 25 cm (9 ins) long. Follow by mulching with garden compost or farmyard manure. There will be no blackberries to pick in the following summer but new canes will be made. Tie these in to the trellis or fence now and then and when they reach the top of the support, pinch them off. They are brittle and easily damaged. If the summer is a dry one, help the bushes to make good growth by watering often. When weeding take care that blackberry roots are not damaged by a hoe or garden fork. Many roots are near the surface. In the second summer after planting your blackberries will bear their first crop; prevent losses to birds by draping and securing old nylon mesh curtains over the bushes when the fruits start to ripen in July or August. When the bushes are established and cropping well you can dispense with these protective covers and share your huge surplus with helpful garden birds just as I do. When the bushes are flowering and fruiting they are also producing new canes on which the following summer's crop will be produced. Tie these new canes loosely to the trellis or fence. As soon as the last ripe berries have been harvested in September or October, untie the canes from which fruit was picked and cut them off as close to the ground as you can. Now untie the new canes and space them at 30 cm (1 ft) or so apart and retie them to replace the old canes you have just pruned away. If you are growing thornless blackberries the old canes can be broken or chopped in sections and added to the compost heap. Never put prickly blackberry pieces on the compost heap. Mulch your blackberry bushes with garden compost each autumn after pruning.

Blackcurrants

John Gerard (English herbalist, 1545–1612) considered blackcurrants as 'of a stinking and somewhat loathing savour'. That is not the opinion of gardeners today of a fruit so highly renowned for its use in jams, jellies and pies, as well as for its high Vitamin C content. This high vitamin content is particularly present in varieties like Laxton's Giant, Raven and Boskoop Giant. Plant blackcurrants in early November when possible. You can, of course, plant at any time during winter but soil conditions are usually better for planting in November. Use a spade to take out holes 1·5–1·8 m (5–6 ft) apart. If you are growing more than a single row leave 1·8 m (6 ft) between rows. When the bushes have reached their full size you will see that they need these wide spacings. Carry out the planting job as for blackberries (see p.

139). After planting, prune back all canes to leave them as short stubs and about 2·5 cm (1 in) above the ground. During early spring inspect the bushes. Firm back into the soil if frost action has loosened them. Mulch with garden compost if this was not

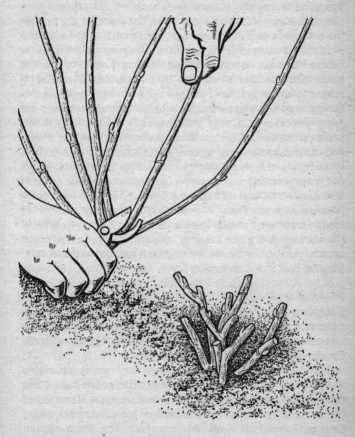

done at planting time. Give water in dry summer weather and mulch the whole area with straw or lawn mowings if possible to keep the weeds down. If you use a hoe to rid the ground of weeds, take care that new growths and near-surface roots are not damaged. In autumn, after leaf fall, cut half the new canes (choose the weaker ones) down to soil level to get the bushes to make stronger new growths. Understanding why, when and how to prune blackcurrants is really important. With blackcurrants you want new, strong shoots from the root system. You do not want bushes made up mainly of older, unfruitful branches. To provide the new canes with adequate room, prune back to soil level two of the older canes after the last fruits have been picked from the bushes in the second year following planting. Thereafter it will be up to you to decide how much of the older growth should be removed after the fruit has been picked. As with so much in gardening there just is no clear rule about blackcurrant pruning; you learn with practice. Always prune back any short, spindly shoots arising from the root system. Birds, probably in search of aphids and other tasty forms of protein, sometimes harm fruit buds in late winter and spring. In very large gardens all soft fruit (fruits not grown as trees) may be grown in a fruit cage, which prevents bird damage to buds and ripening fruits. I had the bud-pecking problem some years ago. To ward off birds (in my case they were house sparrows) I wound black cotton from branch to branch. (Nylon thread is more likely to strangle or cripple birds than cotton.) As soon as the bushes are in full leaf, cut off the cotton. Do not pull it off, otherwise leaves become torn and flowers broken. From now on you need birds to help keep the bushes free from aphids (plant lice) until you take preventive action to keep birds away from the ripening currants. Pick blackcurrants when they are quite black, juicy and softening (the berries will not all ripen at the same time). If harvesting for jam making or for freezing, pick the fruit only in dry weather.

The blackcurrant is the victim of two very common troubles. Most serious is Blackcurrant Gall Mite, often referred to as 'Big Bud' because the mites cause affected buds to swell. If you notice any abnormally swollen buds on your own blackcurrants during early spring, pick them off and burn them. Very badly affected bushes are best grubbed up and burnt. There is no really effective control of this pest. Spraying with lime sulphur and other chemicals is often advised. These sprays are now believed to kill natural predators of the Gall Mites. Always buy young bushes from specialist nurserymen so that your bushes are quite free from this pest.

Reversion is the second unpleasant worry in blackcurrant growing. Affected bushes have leaves which look 'different' from normal, having less veins. Reversion is caused by a virus spread by Blackcurrant Gall Mites. Affected bushes are poor croppers and should be dug up and burnt.

Damsons Plant and cultivate as for plums (see. pp. 149–54).

Gooseberries

When ripe, gooseberries may be pale green, yellow or red depending on the variety; all gooseberries are green when unripe. They can be picked at the unripe stage and follow on after rhubarb in early summer. The picking of a part of the crop can lead to larger, full-ripe gooseberries later. Popular varieties are: Careless (yellow), Lancashire Lad (red), Leveller (yellow), Whinham's Industry (red), Whitesmith (yellow). The gooseberry is an easy, rewarding fruit for the garden or allotment but spreading bushes can finally take up a great deal of space. Because of this I prefer thornless standards. Order bushes for November planting. They can be heeled in if soil conditions are wrong or you have no time to plant them immediately (see p. 131). Plant as for blackberries (see p. 139). Each ordinary (not standard sort) bush should have from two to four branches which, after planting and mulching, should be cut back to half their length and to a bud pointing outwards. Outward-pointing buds develop into outward-growing branches. In gooseberry pruning and training aim at having bushes with open centres so that light and air reach foliage and fruits. Any side shoots on the shortened branches should be pruned back, too, to leave three or four buds. Inspect the young bushes in spring and firm any which have been loosened by frost. Mulch later in spring if a compost or manure mulch were not applied at planting time. Straw or grass mowings may be spread around the area, too, to prevent weed growth and to keep the soil cool and moist. In dry weather water, too, if you feel this may help. Take care if you use a hoe near the bushes that you do not sever near-surface roots. After leaf fall you will see that each bush has from four to eight branches. Prune these back by half their length and to buds pointing outwards. Because gooseberries fruit on one-year-old and two-year-old wood you may prune your bushes by two different methods. For plenty of unripe berries for jam making, bottling or freezing, all you need do as regards pruning is to cut away a complete branch when a bush looks over-crowded with laterals during late autumn or in winter. If the main branches are getting far too long, tip them back by several centimetres, too. For ripe dessert fruit of good size, prune back all laterals (side shoots) in winter to leave them about 5 cm (2 ins) long. In June or July shorten laterals once more to leave them about 12 cm (5 ins) in length.

Earlier I mentioned that I favour standard gooseberries. Mine are now fourteen years old and still cropping well. You can order them from specialist fruit nurserymen, but the number of different varieties is restricted. The prickly gooseberry is grafted on to a tall thornless stem of Golden Currant and looks like a standard rose. Each bush needs only 2·5 sq cm (1 sq in) of soil surface so you may grow bulbs and annual flowers around your gooseberries. Plant standards 1·2 m (4 ft) apart and give each bush a stout tall stake to which you can tie it immediately after planting. Planting and cultivation are as for ordinary bush-type gooseberries, apart from the pruning technique. Aim at having standard bushes open-centred and with about eight permanent branches each from 45–60 cm (18–24 ins) long. In June or July pinch back all side shoots on the branches to leave the laterals 12 cm (5 ins) long. In late autumn or early winter, prune them back to 5 cm (2 ins). Standard gooseberries may be grown in 35-cm (14-in) containers; large tubs are better.

Apart from caterpillars occasionally browsing on the foliage – and you can pick them off – you should not have any worries as regards pests and diseases. American Gooseberry Mildew is said to be common but I have not met up with it. Washing soda is a preventive and is sprayed at the rate of 250 gr ($\frac{1}{2}$ lb) in 10·5 litres (2$\frac{1}{2}$ gallons) of soapy water when the bushes are in flower, when the fruitlets have set and three weeks later. Lime-sulphur is often recommended but should on no account be used on some (sulphur-shy) varieties, notably Leveller. Proprietary fungicides

are also available. Do not confuse this unpleasant gooseberry
trouble with the far commoner European Gooseberry Mildew.
The white mould of this fungus shows on the upper surfaces of
the leaves but seldom attacks the fruit. Allow bushes plenty of
light and air and I doubt whether you will meet up with this
little-to-worry-about mildew.

Loganberry

This bramble is planted and grown in exactly the same way as
blackberries (see pp.138–40). The annual pruning is carried out in
summer because the last fruits to be harvested will be picked
then and not in autumn as with blackberries. The loganberry is of
Californian origin and may not be a success in the coldest parts of
Britain. If you live where winters can be exceptionally cold, ask if
anybody round about has tried growing this fruit. If they haven't
and you wish to try a loganberry, plant it just in front of a south-
facing wall.

The ordinary loganberry (Clone LY59) is prickly. The Thornless Loganberry is equally good cropping-wise and I strongly recommend it for small gardens. Take effective measures against
birds when the first logans are showing pink (see p. 140). When
fully ripe, loganberries are a deep purplish red colour, soft, and
the berries part easily from the 'plug'. Loganberries are never
sweet but children enjoy them raw. Most adults appear to prefer
them after cooking. Like blackberries, logans freeze well and
both of these bramble fruits taste exactly the same as the fresh
fruits if cooked after having been frozen for up to a year. Loganberries have been cultivated in pots at a Kent research station. I
suggest that the thornless sort is an ideal bramble for large pot-
or tub-growing (at least 30 cm or 12 in in diameter) in a backyard,
on a patio or even on a high-rise balcony which gets lots of sunshine. The brambles would need moving to 35-cm (14-in) pots
after two or three years. In the second and subsequent summer
after planting the brambles would benefit from liquid manure or
fertilizer feeds (see p. 66). The bamboo tepee idea suggested for
vegetable marrows (see p. 125) would be an ideal way of supporting pot- or tub-grown brambles.

Pears

Some writers say that pears are more difficult to grow than apples. That is not my opinion, because I found pears to be pest and disease free. All that I have said about site, soil and planting of apples (pp. 130–35) applies with one or two slight differences. Pear trees need more plant foods than apples and a spring mulch of garden compost suits them. Do not try growing pears in grass, as I have suggested for apples. Quince A is the usual rootstock on which pears are grafted these days. Some varieties do not unite well with this rootstock so nurserymen first graft a pear variety which is compatible to the quince rootstock. They then graft the pear they are propagating on to this pear stock. Easiest shape of tree to form and grow is the bush. These should be planted at 4·5 m (15 ft) apart. You may grow peas, beans, root crops, annual flowers during the first and second seasons after planting. Pears are not supposed to do well in colder areas of Britain; if I were gardening in the north, I would grow bush trees where they would have protection from north winds. As I have said about apples – by all means admire pear trees trained as cordons or espaliers and grow them if you know about pruning. Another important point about the pear is its early flowering habit; spring frosts ruin pear blossom. It would be a waste of money and time to plant pears in a frost pocket where the blossom is killed off in two years out of three. Shaping of bush pears follows the pattern suggested for bush apples (see pp. 132–4). When you have your shaped tree, little if any further pruning should be necessary. Young trees benefit from being watered in dry summer weather; established pears may need watering well and often in very dry summer weather in eastern areas of the country. Bush pear trees usually regulate things so that over-bearing does not occur. Only if by some fluke your own pear trees have set far too many fruits should you thin the fruitlets in early July. A heavy crop of fruit on an established tree may weigh the branch down and you may fear it will crack or break under the weight. Pear (and apple) boughs rarely get damaged in this way but to take no chances knock a post or two in the ground and support the branches until the fruit is harvested. Harvesting dessert pears at the right time is something one has to learn. The table below will help you and it also indicates varieties which cross-pollinate. There may be suitable pollinators already around in neighbouring gardens or in a nearby orchard. After harvesting tidy up around the trees as for apples (see p. 135). A general shallow forking of the soil around the trees completes the seasonal work.

Some varieties of pears to choose
Pears for use solely cooked are seldom grown. Most dessert-type may be harvested when hard and green for stewing.

Name	Flowering time	Pick	Use
Beurré Hardy	Late	Oct.	Oct.
Beurré Superfin	Mid-season	Sept./Oct.	Sept./Oct.
Bristol Cross*	Late	Sept./Oct.	Sept./Oct.
Conference†	Mid-season	Oct.	Oct./Nov.
Doyenné du Comice	Late	Oct.	Nov./Dec.
Emile d'Heyst	Mid-season	Oct.	Oct./Nov.
Glou Morceau	Late	Oct.	Dec./Jan.
Gorham	Late	Sept.	Sept.
Josephine de Malines	Mid-season	Oct.	Dec./Jan.
Louise Bonne of Jersey	Early to Mid-season	Oct.	Oct.
Merton Pride	Mid-season	Sept.	Sept.
Packham's Triumph	Mid-season	Oct.	Nov.
Pitmaston Duchess*	Late	Oct.	Oct./Nov.
William's Bon Chrétien‡	Mid-season	Sept.	Sept.

* These two do not produce good pollen. Plant two other different varieties with them. For good pollination of other pears choose another variety which flowers at the same time.
† Considered as the easiest pear to grow.
‡ Pick fruits before they are yellow and ripen them off indoors.

Family trees

As with apples, several varieties of pear can be grafted to provide what are popularly known as 'Family Trees'. At the present time I can find only one combination on offer. This is a single tree bearing William's Bon Chretién, Doyenné du Comice, Conference.

Pear troubles

Although the pear can be subject to about thirty different pests and diseases none should be anticipated, apart from wasps and birds. Here are a few of the possible troubles and something about their prevention.

Canker This is the same fungus which can infect apple trees and is known as *Common* or *Apple Canker*. See p. 136 for treatment.

Scab This is very similar to the Scab of apples and prevention and spraying are as for *Apple Scab* (see p. 138). Do not confuse small dark markings on leaves with Scab spots. Strong winds may bruise and lead to dark marks on young pear foliage.

Birds The merry blackbird and cheerful thrush will peck at ripening pears. Prevent by enclosing the entire tree in small-mesh garden netting.

Wasps The wasp cannot attack hard, unripe pears and the skin of ripening pears is pretty tough. But wasps (and earwigs) will enjoy enlarging any bird pecks. Take precautions against birds and, if you fear wasp damage, tie each ripening pear in a perforated, transparent polythene fruit bag. Finding and destroying wasp nests is often advocated. Bear in mind, too, that the wasp is the friend and ally of the gardener in spring when this insect devours aphids (greenfly, blackfly).

Fire Blight This bacterial disease was first noted in Britain in 1957. Affected blossom blackens and dies. The foliage appears scorched; trees die. If you suspect that you have a tree suffering from this disease you are bound by law to notify the local officer of the National Agricultural Advisory Service or the Plant Pathology Laboratory, Hatching Green, Harpenden, Herts.

Brown Rot This fungus also attacks apples and plums and is described on p. 136. On pears it is more likely to occur where wasps, earwigs or birds have already caused a wound on a fruit.

Plums

The gardener who grows plums can pick each fruit in perfect, soft-ripe condition, dripping with sweetness but not a soggy mess. A recently published encyclopedia lists over forty different plums. Nurserymen may offer about a dozen and the gardener may have heard of none of them apart form Victoria. Although you will find a short list of plum varieties on pp. 151–2, I suggest, provided that you have no other personal preference, that you choose Victoria. Fruits are yellow and red and large, crops can be excellent and this variety is dual-purpose: for dessert, jams or bottling. Victoria is also self-pollinating; of course if plum trees with compatible pollen are in the vicinity, pollen transferred by bees to your own Victoria tree may well increase the total crop. Unfortunately, a spring frost can kill Victoria blossom. If you live where frost damage to plum blossom is a known hazard then I suggest the hardy, reliable and self-fertile cooking plum Czar. The fruits of this variety may be eaten raw when absolutely ripe but they lack the flavour and cooking quality of Victoria. Training plums as fan-shaped trees on walls, which can give some protection against spring frost and also radiate heat to assist ripening, is often suggested to gardeners with gardens in cold, exposed positions. But the training and pruning of fruit trees to any restricted form does call for quite a bit of knowledge so I recommend bush trees. Like all fruits, plum trees need good drainage but a soil which does not dry out rapidly in a period of summer drought. Although plums do not do well in a soil which is very chalky, lime must be present. If you sprinkle a little lime over layers of refuse as you add them to the compost heap, your plum trees will not need any further lime dressings. But if your soil is on the acid side and you feel that your plums would crop far better if more calcium were present in the soil, spread ground chalk (carbonate of lime) at the rate of 500 gr per sq m (1 lb per sq yd) around the trees one autumn. Do not repeat the dosage. Excess lime can lead to a soil having a deficiency of trace elements.

St Julien A is considered as about the best rootstock for plums in the garden but when investing in one or more plums it is really far better to leave the choice of rootstock to the nurseryman. If you tell him you want a bush plum and explain to him fairly roughly the sort of soil you have, he, as a specialist, will provide a tree with the rootstock he considers best for your particular circumstances. Plums like plenty of sunshine; they also need plenty of good food. Never try growing plums in grass, such as in the middle of a lawn. The fertile soil of the vegetable garden suits plums but it would be unwise to have a tree near one's vegetables where digging and hoeing would disturb the shallow feeding roots of plum trees. Plant plum trees in November if possible, or during the winter when soil conditions permit. Planting is as for apples (see pp. 131–4) with trees spaced 4·5 m (15 ft) apart. By all means grow root crops, peas, beans and other vegetables in the wide space between young plum trees.

The plum is very susceptible to a disease called Silver Leaf (see p. 153) and any pruning during the dormant period leaves wounds through which this fungus may enter. So, after planting a maiden plum, delay the initial pruning (see pp. 132 ff.) until the spring when maidens should be pruned back to leave them 90 cm (3 ft) tall. If there are any laterals (side shoots) on maidens after this pruning, leave them to grow for a couple of years before cutting them off so that the trees then have their desirable bare trunks. If you have bought and planted two- or three-year-old trees already partially trained by the nurseryman as bush trees, only continue the training and pruning when the trees have settled down well, within a year or so. Keep down weeds round plum trees but never use a spade or garden fork near them or you will almost certainly either sever or damage the many shallow roots which stretch out beneath the trees. To ensure that young plum trees make continuous, steady growth in dry summer weather, give plenty of water. In a very dry summer (particularly in eastern England) well-established plum trees benefit from heavy waterings, too. With established plums do not prune at all unless it is absolutely necessary. Always trim back to healthy wood any shoots which appear quite dead in summer. If any large branches have to be removed because they are partially dead or chafing other branches, or because the tree is overcrowded with branches, saw them off cleanly in June or July. Seal the wounds with a tree sealing compound or white lead paint. If you inherit an ancient plum, give it a couple of seasons to show what it can do. If the crops are poor or if the tree just looks sick, grub it up and burn it. If the tree has cropped reasonably well and would probably benefit from pruning, saw off some of the oldest branches in summer and paint the wounds to encourage the tree to produce new fruiting wood. Every few years established plum trees (particularly Victoria) can set a tremendous crop; thinning the fruitlets is quite a task and you may be eager to have as many plums as your tree can mature. But plum boughs often crack under the weight of crop and cracked or broken boughs invite Silver Leaf fungus. Prevent this trouble by shoring up heavily-laden, drooping boughs in July. Pick ripe plums when they are fully coloured and soft. Take care, though, if you are growing any of the very thin-skinned yellow plums that they do not split on the tree, otherwise every wasp in the parish will smell out your crop and you will wish you had picked the plums a week earlier. After the last plums have been harvested, tidy up around the tree, consigning any windfall plums and other debris to the compost heap. Then apply a mulch of garden compost at the rate of a good barrow load to the square metre (square yard). If there is no compost ready in late summer, apply it in the autumn or in the following May.

Some varieties of plums to choose

The varieties listed here are generally recommended for planting by the amateur gardener and are likely to do well where growing conditions are right.

Name	Flowering time	Pick	Remarks
Early Laxton†	Early	Late July	Yellow, flushed red. Fine cooker and quite good eaten raw
Denniston's Superb*	Early	Mid Aug.	Yellowish-green. Good for eating raw or for cooking

Name	Flowering time	Pick	Remarks
Victoria*	Mid-season	Mid to late Aug.	Large, yellow and red. Best all-purpose plum
Ouillins Gage* *syn.* Ouillins Golden Gage	Late	Mid Aug.	Large, golden yellow. Dessert or cooking
Jefferson†	Early	Early Sept.	Golden yellow with red spots. Ideal for dessert use
Severn Cross*	Early	Late Sept.	Large, oval, golden with pink flush. First-class eater and cooker
Czar*	Late	Early Aug.	Purple-black, medium size. Cooker. Recommended for exposed and frosty gardens
Yellow Pershore* ('Yellow Egg')	Late	Aug.–Sept.	Yellow, medium-sized plum recommended for jams and bottling
Purple Pershore*	Mid-season	Aug.	Medium-sized deep purple plum noted for hardiness. Good cooking quality
Early Rivers† (Rivers Early Prolific)	Early	Late July–Aug.	Small to medium, purple-black plum recommended for culinary use. When fully-ripe makes good eating raw

* Self-fertile.
† Needs a pollinator – another of the early flowering plums listed here.

Damsons are grown in exactly the same manner as plums. Merry-weather, a popular, large damson, is self-fertile.

Plum troubles

Many garden plum trees remain trouble-free all their lives. But the plum is subject to two dozen different pests and diseases. Here are a few of the more common troubles.

Aphids Three species of aphids (greenfly, blackfly) attack plum foliage. Most common is Leaf-curling plum aphis, appearing on young leaves in spring. Leaf curl occurs and new young shoots are damaged. The aphids leave the trees in April and spend the summer on clover and other flowering plants. A winged generation returns to lay eggs on plum trees in autumn. The overwintering eggs can be destroyed by a tar-oil wash applied before late January. Derris, applied as a spray, may also be used at budburst and again in early April. Do not spray at blossom time when bees and other pollinators are on the trees.

Birds Bullfinches and house sparrows attack buds in winter, possibly searching for aphids. Black cotton wound among the branches is a deterrent; a fruit cage gives complete protection. Pieces of shiny tin-plate suspended from the branches can deter birds. Unripe plums are not attacked by them; ripe and ripening plums are. Covering an entire tree with small garden mesh is one answer. Tying each choice plum in a clear, perforated polythene bag is another.

Brown Rot This fungus also attacks apples and pears and is described on p. 136. Take action as suggested for Brown Rot on apples (see p. 136).

Silver Leaf First recorded outbreak of this fungal disease in Britain was reported in 1902. It is now the most serious plum disease. The fungal spores are wind-borne and gain entry via a wound or pruning cut. The disease can spread rapidly throughout the tree. Leaves take on a silvery hue. A brown staining shows when a branch is cut. Fungal fruiting bodies, yellow above and purple beneath, may appear on the bark. The natural flow of sap seals wounds rapidly during the months of June, July and August, so that is the time when any pruning should be done. If growing conditions are good, vigorous trees can recover from a slight attack of Silver Leaf. Czar and Victoria are very susceptible to the disease so support heavy branches to prevent cracking or breaking which allow the fungi to enter. Any branches showing Silver Leaf should be sawn off and burnt before 15 July in accordance with a Government order. Trees which are badly infected must be grubbed up and burned.

Wasps These will enlarge any bird pecks on ripe and ripening plums and also devour any split, ripe plums. To make the traditional wasp trap, mix some jam or treacle in beer, half-fill a jam jar with the mixture, fix a paper lid on top. Make holes in the paper to allow wasps to enter and hang the trap in a plum tree. Alternatively, tie choice dessert plums at the ripening stage in clear, perforated polythene fruit bags. Water generously in dry weather; the thin-skinned yellow plums are more likely to split than plums with thicker skins. Pick off any bird-pecked plums.

Raspberries

Although quite commonly grown in gardens, raspberries are not often grown well so that poor crops result. Starting off with 'clean' stock is very important. It is a waste of cash, time and labour, investing in stock which is infected with one or more of the weakening virus diseases which beset the raspberry. Specialist nurserymen do their best to ensure that the raspberries they offer are as free from virus troubles as is possible. Consult the list of varieties on pp. 158–9.

Lloyd George is considered to be the best-flavoured raspberry yet introduced, but unfortunately it degenerates quite rapidly through virus infections; if it does not do as well as you had hoped do not blame soil or growing conditions. The newer Malling raspberries are mentioned in the list but, as they have been grown so far on a research trial basis, they may not turn out to be so remarkably good under our less favourable garden conditions. Because raspberries are permanent garden features – permanent means up to eight years at least – and because they are greedy, it is pretty senseless planting them in low fertility soils. Planting raspberries or any other permanent subjects in a garden infested with perennial weeds is also unwise. If you have recently taken over a very weedy garden or allotment grow vegetables for a year or two before planting any permanent subjects (see Chapter 1).

Good drainage is as important for raspberries as it is for almost every garden food crop. Heavy soils are ideal because they retain needed water in very dry summers. Light soils must have their humus content increased so that the water-holding capacity is greatly improved. Chalky soils also need heavy dressings of garden compost dug into them. Even then there is the chance that the raspberries will not do well because they prefer slightly acidic soils and not soils with a high chalk content. November is the correct time to plant. Choose a sunny position and ideally rows should run from north to south so that each side of a row receives its full quota of summer sun. Before planting fork over the site to a depth of 12–15 cm (5–6 ins). Then, take out a trench 15 cm (6 in) deep and 30 cm (12 in) wide, using a spade. Rows should be 1·8 m (6 ft) apart. Plant the young canes at approximately 45 cm (18 ins) apart, spreading out the roots and taking care that the soil mark (see p. 132) is at the correct position. Plant very firmly but take care that no young white buds at the bases of the canes are damaged. After planting, mulch with garden compost and some straw if you have any. Nurserymen used to be rather keen to supply unpruned young canes so that customers would feel they were getting their money's worth. But with today's postal rates it is probable that nurserymen will carry out initial pruning before packing and mailing canes. After all, the long canes have to be pruned back to leave the newly-planted raspberries no taller than 30 cm (1 ft). If you receive raspberries which have not been pruned, cut them back; break the unwanted pieces of canes into small sections and add them to the compost pile. Supports are needed. Erect two strong 2-m (7-ft) posts at 60 cm (2 ft) apart and at either end of each row; 60 cm (2 ft) of each post is hammered into the ground. If a row is longer than about 3·5 m (12 ft), similar posts need erecting at every 3·5 m (12 ft). The posts are linked with wires at 45 cm (18 ins), 90 cm (3 ft) and 1·5 m (4 ft 6 ins) above soil level. The supports should be in position by the May following planting. As the raspberry canes grow make sure they are within the wire box trellis. Tie the canes to the trellis with soft string to prevent bruising of canes and foliage if rasp-

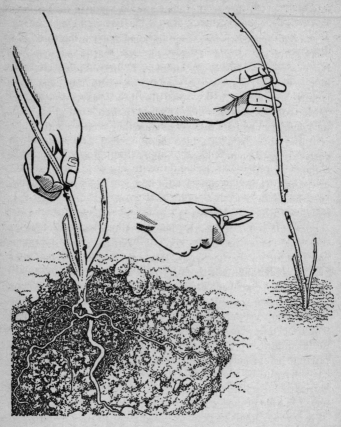

berries are planted in a windy position. In early spring firm any
canes planted in the previous November which have been loosened
by frosts. Aim now to help your raspberries to settle down and
make a good rooting system and a few strong canes. If mulching
with garden compost was not done at planting time, mulch in
May. Do any necessary weeding and watering throughout the
season but do take care if you use a hoe not to damage near-soil
surface roots. Never use a spade around raspberries; if you use a
garden fork during annual digging, use it to a depth of only a few

centimetres. The raspberry fruits on wood made in the previous summer so do not expect any fruit in the summer after planting. Tidy up around the canes in autumn and apply a mulch of garden compost or strawy farmyard manure. Mulching annually is worthwhile with raspberries. The canes will need tipping annually in late February or early March; prune back any very tall canes to leave them 1·5 m (5 ft) long. Prune back shorter canes by 7·5–10 cm (3–4 ins). During late spring new young canes will start to grow from the roots. Tuck these into the 'box' as they grow; tie them to the wires in very windy gardens. Fruits on canes which have been denied water are dry, pippy and unpalatable. A mulch of straw or lawn mowings laid down in June or in early July can help keep the ground moist and save you watering regularly. Raspberries flower late so that frost damage to the blossom is rare, even if your garden or allotment is a noted frost pocket.

Bees pollinate raspberry flowers and the green fruitlets ripen rapidly in July. Wasps are not a problem but birds can be a nuisance. If you grow your raspberries by the wire box method I have suggested, it is easy to enclose the whole row within small-mesh garden netting when the first raspberries are just turning pink. To prevent birds from slipping under the netting at soil level, thread 90-cm (3-ft) or 1·5-m (5-ft) bamboo canes through the mesh of the nets at ground level. When harvesting I raise the netting and lodge it at the top of the 'box' and replace the nets immediately after picking. If raspberries are wanted for bottling, jam making or freezing, pick them on a dry day. The raspberry season lasts for about three weeks. As soon as the last of the crop has been harvested and protective netting has been removed, it is time to carry out annual pruning; cut off as near soil level as possible all canes from which fruit has been picked and transfer them to the compost heap. Any weak, short new canes should also be removed similarly. With established raspberries leave only five or six strong, new canes on each *stool* (the clump which develops from each of the original canes you planted) to replace the old canes. In a very dry summer give the raspberry rows a good drenching with water periodically to prevent a shortage of soil moisture hindering the production of good, new canes. If you have a home freezer I strongly recommend you to grow

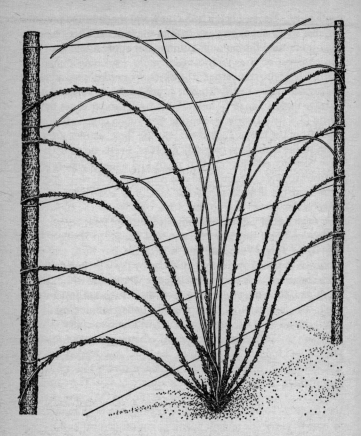

raspberries. The frozen fruit may, of course, be stewed, eaten with cream or added to tarts and pies. From raspberries in the garden or on the allotment you can make real raspberry jam, so different from the raspberry jam on sale.

Some varieties of raspberries to choose

Malling Admiral (New) Ripens at about the same time as the older Norfolk Giant and better cropping than this variety, with larger fruits of better quality, too. The fruit is borne on rather long side growths which may be damaged if this raspberry is planted in a windy situation. No virus symptoms have been noticed on this new raspberry as yet.

Malling Delight (New) Early-ripening and has Lloyd George in its ancestry. Very heavy cropper. The raspberries are large and rather light pink in colour. Tends to resist some viruses.

Malling Promise Noted for early ripening, flavour and good quality and for heavy cropping. Very vigorous grower and cane growth must be controlled by the digging up of the many new canes which may start to grow outside of the rows proper.

Malling Exploit Early ripening and similar to Malling Promise. The raspberries can be very large.

Malling Jewel Recommended for Scotland and northern England. Early to mid season and a good cropper. Less liable to suffer from wind damage than most varieties.

Malling Enterprise Mid season. Good as regards flavour and crops. Large raspberries. A favourite for jam making.

Malling Orion (New) Late mid season variety ripening after Malling Delight. Short, conical fruits of good flavour. Good cropper. Resists viruses. Has Lloyd George in its ancestry.

Lloyd George Considered to be the best raspberry for flavour. Crops over a long period and often produces a second, small crop on the new canes in autumn. Unfortunately, Lloyd George so often falls victim quickly to virus diseases.

Norfolk Giant Late ripening, medium sized, somewhat acidic, purplish raspberries. The crop continues into August. Do not plant this variety where there is risk of frost damage to the flowers. Does not do well in all localities.

Glen Clova Has become increasingly popular since its introduction a few years ago. Noted for heavy cropping, fine flavour and firmness of berry.

Golden Everest Typical of the few yellow-fruited raspberries still around. These are very seldom grown by gardeners because red raspberries are the general preference, but the yellows are sweeter and are excellent for dessert use.

Raspberry troubles

Mention has been made of weakening virus diseases (see p. 154) and the importance of starting off with 'clean' stock has been emphasized. If your raspberry canes get shorter and your crops poorer, you can be sure that weakening virus troubles are the cause. Grub up and burn the lot. Start off with fresh stock planted in a different part of the garden or allotment. Perhaps the new Malling raspberries will remain resistant to the more common virus strains, but only time will tell. If you fear that the occasional ripe raspberry may contain a small white grub of the Raspberry Beetle, inspect each batch of fruit after picking. Any grubs climb on to the surface of the harvested berries. Only if you have been plagued with Raspberry Beetle should you spray with derris as a precautionary measure when the first berries are beginning to colour. Do not spray until late evening when bees are less active. Derris is harmless to man and his pets – except pool fish.

Strawberries

The modern strawberry is very much a man-made production and although the most delicious of garden fruits and so easy to grow, the plants often pick up virus diseases which weaken and distort them. Crops from badly-infected plants are poor and the strawberries are small and often of bad shape. Plants may not remain perfectly healthy after three or four years and should be grubbed up and burnt; start off again with fresh, 'clean' stock bought from a reputable supplier. Apart from the alpines (see p. 166) you start off with plants. A choice of varieties is given on pp. 167–8. Early summer or June fruiters are the best known, but you can now have strawberries from June until October.

Good soil drainage is vital with strawberries. Poor drainage can lead to all sorts of strange, plant-killing troubles. Sunshine is also a requirement and so is plant food. Never lime soil where you are about to plant strawberries but choose a spot where the soil is absolutely fertile. When farmers used far more animal manure than they usually do these days, 50 tons was not considered an exceptional dressing per acre on land being prepared for strawberry planting. Modern research has proved that strawberry plants do not benefit all that much from food applied to the growing plants. They want the food in the soil itself. If you can spread garden compost over the site and set the young plants in this thick, rich mulch, so much the better. Light soils dry out rapidly and unless they are packed with humus (the final end-product of decayed manure or garden compost), they dry out quickly in a good summer. Strawberries from plants which are short of water at the roots have a mauve tinge; they are also dry and no amount of cream can make them palatable. A sandy soil into which garden compost has been dug for a few years can often hold sufficient water for the production of early summer strawberries, but can never supply the needs, water-wise, of late summer/autumn fruiters. It is up to you to give the additional water. I find it best to poke the spout of a watering can close to the soil which prevents the wetting and possibly rotting of ripening strawberries.

Planting time for strawberries varies. To have ripe strawberries next June order young plants for planting in late July or in August. If they are pot-grown plants, so much the better. If the nurseryman cannot deliver earlier than September or early October insist on pot-grown plants only. If you plant plants raised in open ground (young plants not propagated in pots), in autumn they will not have made sufficient root growth to produce a fair crop of fruit by the following June. June fruiters may also be planted at any time during winter when soil conditions permit. But here again the plants will have little time to settle down to fruiting. With late summer/autumn fruiters there is no need at all to invest in the more expensive pot-raised plants. Open-ground runner plants should be planted in October or November if you can; or in winter or early spring if soil conditions permit. Always plant strawberries as quickly as possible after you take delivery of the plants. The first batch of flowers (produced in May or June) is always pinched off late summer/autumn fruiters; if you leave them on there will be a few fruits in June and a miserable main crop. The planting technique with strawberries varies, depending on whether you are planting pot-raised or open-ground runner plants. Do not disturb the rooting system of pot-grown plants. Remove plants carefully from clay or plastic pots. Tear off polythene film pots and tear off, too, any dry parts of card or paper pots. Pots made of a man-made fibre are best cut away, as strawberry roots just cannot pass through the mesh and are stunted because of the tightly packed, poor rooting system. Open-ground runner plants are treated quite differently. Their roots are usually washed by the supplier and need to be spread out in the planting holes. It is a mistake to set strawberry plants deeply in the ground but essential to plant them firmly. Using a garden line ensures that you have straight rows. Planting distances vary depending on your choice of strawberry cultivation. Plants in single rows are usually set at 38–45 cm (15–18 ins) between plants, with rows 75 cm (30 ins) apart. If you want an extra early or a late crop and are using cloche protection, more room will be needed than the conventional planting distance of 75 cm (30 ins) between the rows. If cloches are not going to be used for an extra late crop, late summer/autumn fruiters are best planted in double staggered rows. Space plants 38 cm (15 ins) apart in the double rows and leave 90 cm (3 ft) between each block of double rows. Early summer (not to be cloched) plants may be set out at these same spacings if you wish to grow the plants by the matted bed system.

Here is how June/July fruiters are cultivated by the matted bed method. Plants are set out 38 cm (15 ins) apart in beds. Each bed is 90 cm (3 ft) from the next and the two staggered rows in each bed are 38 cm (15 ins) apart. During the first and second summers, allow the plants to root cadet (small runner plants) plants around them so that the whole bed gets jammed tight with plants and there is little room for weeds. The ripening fruits topple on to the strawberry leaves and most remain clean. In the third and fourth seasons you pinch off all runners from all the plants to prevent more cadet plant formation; if a few plants could do with more space, use a handfork or a trowel to remove a nearby plant and so prevent congestion. At the end of the fourth season you dig up the entire bed and start off with new stock plants in a different part of the garden.

Late summer/autumn strawberries are often referred to as 'remontants' in the gardening press and in books; American gardeners call them 'everbearers'. They are always cultivated by the matted bed system. La Sans Rivale makes lots of cadet plants; Gento makes relatively few. It would be difficult to retain cadet plants of La Sans Rivale within the confines of a row to be cloched in September, so Gento would be a better choice. With remontant varieties which grow many cadet plants around the parent plants in one single season, the entire bed should be dug up in November; small cadet plants which have not flowered should be replanted in a new bed elsewhere in the garden and the rest of the plants put on the compost heap. Remontants which make relatively few cadet plants each season can be left alone for three or four seasons, by which time you will be considering investing in new stock plants so you can dig up the entire bed, consign the

plants to the compost heap or the bonfire, make a fresh bed elsewhere and plant fresh stock plants. With the matted bed system
you encourage cadet plants to root by pinning them (using a
piece of 'U'-shaped wire) to the ground.

General cultivation of established early
summer strawberries

In April and in May hoe between plants being grown in single
rows and hoe, too, between matted beds. A handfork is the best
tool to use on matted beds. The plants start flowering in May. If
you intend to keep the fruits clean, only tuck a little straw beneath
the fruit clusters after the berries are well-formed; many flowers
can be blackened by frost if the straw is laid in position during the
flowering period. If your plants are being cultivated by the matted
bed system you will want cadet plants. These form on *runners* or
stolons (horizontal stems produced by strawberry plants in
summer). If your plants are growing in single rows, you will not
want them cluttered up with cadet plants, so pinch off all runners
on and off throughout the summer season. As soon as the first
berries are showing pink coloration, erect netting or you may lose
the entire crop to birds. Strawberries do not ripen off if picked
under-ripe so pick the fully ripe fruit almost daily. After the last
strawberries have been harvested, remove the nets, tidy up generally and if you feel it time to buy in fresh stock plants, dig up
the old plants and put them on the compost heap or the bonfire.

General cultivation of late summer/autumn
(remontant) strawberries

In April and May loosen soil around the beds and remove weed
seedlings. If you have started off with small plants set out in the
previous winter or a month or so ago, pinch off all flower buds as
soon as you see them in late April, May and June. After one or
more seasons there is no need to do this but do not expect a large
crop of ripe strawberries in June. Tuck straw, if you wish – and if
the bed is not too matted to do so – beneath the ripening strawberries in July. Unfortunately, in a very wet season, using straw
can lead to the loss of a lot of ripe fruit due to fungal rots. Net the

rows or beds to prevent loss of fruits to birds. Pick the ripe fruit at least twice each week between late July or early August until late September. For continued good fruiting in October remove the nets and set cloches or movable frames over the plants in September when the weather begins to feel chilly at night, and continue picking regularly during October; pick the occasional punnet of ripe fruit from unprotected plants. Remove cloches, frames or nets from plants in November. Tidy up generally or (if you wish) dig up all of the plants and replant small rooted runner plants elsewhere.

Strawberry plants in containers

For the gardener with no real garden at all the strawberry is one of the few garden fruits which may be successfully cultivated in pots, tubs and other containers. Choose early summer fruiters. Use, when possible, a mixture of good top soil and garden compost (50 : 50) in the containers. Levington Potting or a similar compost may be used instead but makes strawberry growing rather expensive. The barrel method of strawberry growing should also be considered. You need a large barrel. Wooden barrels with suitable holes are usually used but I see no reason why steel barrels should not be used, too. If you get a barrel and make the holes yourself do not forget to drill a few 2·5-cm (1-in) diameter holes in the base of the barrel for drainage purposes. Holes in which strawberry plants will grow should be 6 cm (2½ ins) in diameter. Stand the barrel on a couple of house bricks and put a 5-cm (2-in) layer of broken clay pots, brick rubble or large stones into the barrel before filling it with a mixture of soil and garden compost. Fill to the first row of planting holes and firm the compost well. Set the first row of plants in position and cover their roots with the soil/compost mixture. Firm again. Now insert a length of drainpipe 15 cm (6 ins) in diameter vertically in the centre of the barrel. Continue filling the barrel and setting plants in position. At the same time, drop pieces of broken brick or large stones into the pipe, raising it now and then as more plants are put in position. After the top row of plants has been planted, remove the pipe to leave the core of rough drainage material. Spread the soil/compost mixture thickly over the surface of the barrel and plant six strawberries in

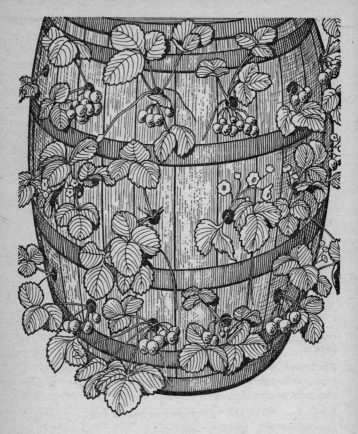

it. Always keep the barrel well-watered in dry weather between spring and autumn. Liquid feeds (see p. 66) should be applied to container-grown plants when fruits are swelling during the third and fourth seasons after planting. Keep all runners (stolons) pinched off regularly throughout the summer.

Alpine strawberries

The fruits are small and dry and do not make good eating until soaked with white wine, dressed with cream and eaten as the luxury dessert 'fraises des bois'. Baron Solemacher is the popular alpine. Plants are on sale or you can raise your own from seeds in pots or trays in an unheated greenhouse in September or March, or outdoors in April. Allow 30 cm (12 ins) between plants in the garden. A good place for alpines is alongside the garden path; they can replace lobelia in the flower garden. Alpines also do well in pots and window-boxes. There are no stolons to pinch off and birds are unlikely to consider the dry fruits of interest. The fruits are not likely to topple on to the soil or compost so do not bother to use straw. Alpines produce a small crop of ripe fruit in June followed by flushes of more fruits in July, August and even September. Discard the plants after they have borne fruit for two seasons. You can use seeds taken from your own ripe alpines. Do not be surprised if the occasional alpine plant presents you with a crop of white instead of the conventional red alpines.

Some varieties of strawberries to choose

Baron Solemacher (JJ) (JO)* Runnerless alpine. Compact bushy plants with light green foliage. Fruits are small, conical and dry.

Cambridge Favourite (JJ) Vigorous and heavy cropping. Fruits are bright red, evenly-shaped, conical, handsome. Fair, sweet flavour.

Cambridge Rival (JJ) Crops well over a short period. Large fruits, wedge-shaped or conical. Very good flavour. Does well in wetter parts of the country.

Cambridge Vigour (JJ) Good cropper, medium sized, conical, glossy red berries. Good flavour.

Elista (JJ) Crops well. Bright red, rounded, even berries of good flavour. Plants are compact and may be set out as close as 22 cm (9 ins) apart in the rows.

Gento (JO) Medium to large, bright red, cone-shaped berries of good flavour. Crops well. Makes relatively few cadet plants.

Grandee (JJ) Rounded, handsome bright red, large strawberries of good flavour. The heaviest crop is in the second season after planting.

Redgauntlet (JJ) A heavy cropper of large, deep red berries with white flesh tinged red. Not renowned for its flavour.

Red Rich (JO) Fairly good cropper; berries are bright to deep red and of medium size. Makes relatively few cadets.

Royal Sovereign (JJ) Large, wedge-shaped or conical, bright red strawberries and deliciously sweet. Plants can crop well but are liable to rather quick virus debility.

St Claude (JO) Good cropper of handsome, bright red fruit. Makes many cadet plants. Hampshire Maid is probably a selection of St Claude.

Talisman (JJ) Vigorous, heavy cropper. Berries are deep red and of medium size. Latest ripening of the early summer strawberries.

La Sans Rivale (JO) Very vigorous and plants need plenty of space. Makes many cadet plants. Berries are bright red, conical and with sweet pink flesh.

Tamella (JJ) A new Dutch strawberry. Large wedge-shaped, juicy, fine flavoured berries.

* JJ = June/July fruiting; JO = Late July/October fruiting.

Strawberry troubles

I have grown strawberries for more than twenty-five years and the only troubles I have had with this fruit are:

Birds The answer is to net plants just as soon as the first strawberry starts to change from green to pink.

Slugs A normal hazard of strawberry growing and not a worry unless straw is laid down and the season then turns out to be a wet one.

Grey Mould Ripe and unripe berries turn brown and rot. They become covered with a grey, powdery mould. Common in October. Common, too, in a wet summer. Pick off all affected fruits.

Virus infections Plants are dwarfed; the leaves may be crinkled and of poor colour; crops are bad. Dig up plants and buy fresh stock. Always invest in new stock after the third or fourth season unless, of course, you are fortunate and your plants show continued good health and cropping potential. Viruses are in the sap of the plants where no chemical spray can get at them and are transmitted from plant to plant by aphids (greenfly). Recommendations that one should spray regularly with pesticides to discourage and kill aphids – which, by the way, I have never seen on my own strawberry plants, – appear naïve to me. After all, one of the blessings in growing one's own fruit and vegetables is to have produce which has not been kept going by chemical sprays.

Appendix 1

Suggested books for further reading

Grow Your Own Fruit and Vegetables by Lawrence D. Hills (Faber and Faber)

Soft Fruit Growing by E. G. Gilbert (Penguin Books)

The Vegetable Grower's Handbook by Arthur J. Simons (Penguin Books)

Less Usual Vegetables by Brian Furner (Macdonald and Janes)

Herbs for Health and Cookery by Claire Loewenfeld and Philippa Back (Pan Books)

An Agricultural Testament by Sir Albert Howard (Oxford University Press)

Farming and Gardening for Health or Disease by Sir Albert Howard (Faber and Faber)

Practical Organic Gardening by Ben Easey (Faber and Faber)

The Book of Herbs by Dorothy Hall (George Allen & Unwin and Pan Books)

Complete Book of Home Freezing by Audrey Ellis (Hamlyn)

Deep-Freeze Cookery by Marika Hanbury Tenison (Pan Books)

Deep-Freeze Sense by Marika Hanbury Tenison (Pan Books)

British gardening magazines

Amateur Gardening, Popular Gardening, Garden News (weekly), *Practical Gardening, Garden* (monthly)

Appendix 2

Sources of supply
Vegetable seeds – mail order seedsmen
Alexander & Brown, The Scottish Seed House, Perth
Samuel Dobie & Son Ltd, Upper Dee Mills, Llangollen LL20 8SD
S. E. Marshall & Co. Ltd, Oldfield Lane, Wisbech, Cambs
Suttons Seeds, Hele Road, Torquay TQ2 7QJ
Thompson & Morgan (Ipswich) Ltd, London Road, Ipswich
 IP2 0BA
W. J. Unwin Ltd, Histon, Cambridge
G. Winfield & Son Ltd, 26 Westgate Street, Gloucester GL1 2NH
All of the above offer seeds of some garden herbs. The following
specialize in the supply of herb seeds and plants by mail order:
Dorwest Herb Growers, Shipton Gorge, Bridport, Dorset
E. & A. Evetts, Ashfields Herb Nursery, Hinstock, Market Drayton,
 Salop

Fruit trees, bushes and strawberry plants
by mail order
Bees Ltd, Sealand, Chester CH1 6BA
Blackmoor Nurseries, Blackmoor, Liss, Hants GU33 6BS
Rivers, The Nurseries, Sawbridgeworth, Herts CM21 0HJ
F. Toynbee Ltd, Barnham, Bognor Regis, Sussex
Hillier & Sons, Winchester
Ken Muir, Honeypot Farm, Weeley Heath, Clacton-on-Sea, Essex
 CO16 9BJ (not tree fruits)

Green manures and Huker compost bin
Henry Doubleday Research Association, Convent Lane, Bocking,
 Braintree, Essex

For help and advice

Local help may be obtainable from your Parks Department or the Town Clerk's office. If you live way out in the country, your County Hall is worth contacting. The county authority will probably have an advisory officer willing to help you. Four of the gardening magazines offer a free advisory service to readers. Fellows of the Royal Horticultural Society can get advice from the London office or from the Society's Garden at Wisley, Surrey. If you need advice about compost making, green manures and pesticides the Henry Doubleday Research Association can help you whether you live in the United Kingdom or abroad (see p. 171 for address). The National Vegetable Society publishes an annual Handbook; the Secretary's name and address are: Mr S. J. Collins, 55 The Drive, Isleworth, Middlesex. The Soil Association, Walnut Tree Manor, Haughley, Suffolk, has Groups in many parts of the country. This society sells books on the production of home-grown food. The National Society of Leisure Gardeners, 22 High Street, Flitwick, Bedfordshire, takes special interest in the welfare of allotment holders.

If you wish to see all kinds of fruits, vegetables and herbs in gardening surroundings, visit the Garden of the Royal Horticultural Society, Wisley, Surrey. No charge is made to Fellows; the public has to pay an entrance fee. If you are a keen gardener you may become a Fellow of the Society. Write for details to the Royal Horticultural Society, Vincent Square, London SW1P 2PE. Make good use of the local library; they can get hold of books which are no longer in print such as the two Albert Howard works listed in Appendix 1.

Appendix 3

Your seed order

To help the mail order seedsman:

(*a*) Where possible use the order form supplied with the annual seed catalogue.

(*b*) Send off your seed order in January; February at latest.

(*c*) Do not forget to enclose the total payment including any postage and packing.

(*d*) Check that you have written your name and address in block letters on the seed order form.

To help yourself:

(*a*) Discuss the order with your wife. She will not want to have produce which nobody in the family cares for. Not everybody likes parsnips, for example; some families do not eat vegetable marrow.

(*b*) Do not over-order. Try to work out approximately how many rows of each vegetable you will be able to grow in your limited garden or allotment space.

(*c*) Prevent gluts. Summer cabbage is excellent but seldom much relished when French or runner beans are in the garden. A row of lettuce is excellent if the family eats at least one a day in summer but two rows of lettuce can be an embarrassment if you have to give one row away and the site could have been used for another wanted vegetable.

(*d*) Older, better known varieties are always worth selecting. Choose where possible varieties known to do well in neighbouring gardens and allotments. But a new variety (called a novelty by seedsmen) is worth trying. It may have hybrid vigour, may resist a common disease, may be hardier. Always be prepared to try out at least one novelty each season.

(*e*) Do not order seeds of a vegetable which has some special requirement which you lack. Example: Do not order greenhouse sort cucumbers if you intend growing cucumbers in the open garden. Choose a hardier variety.

(*f*) If you can buy shallots, onion sets and seed potatoes locally this will be cheaper than buying them from a mail order supplier and paying postage.

(*g*) If you have a home freezer, look for special remarks in seed catalogues about varieties of special merit for freezing.

(*h*) Postal charges may be lower if you ask fellow gardeners if you can order seeds for them, too. Postal charges on several orders may work out more cheaply for each of you.

(*i*) On allotment sites seed potatoes and vegetable seeds are sometimes ordered in bulk. Enquire on your allotment site about this. Bulk buying can reduce postal and other carriage charges. With seed potatoes, it is usually cheaper to buy several hundred kilograms in bulk than in small lots of 6 and 12 kg (14 and 28 lb).

Your vegetable seed order

The seed order here covers the more usually grown vegetables. Except where stated, 1 packet of seed is ample for each vegetable. Add to your order any special requirements you may have, and check on carriage or postal charges if applicable (see catalogues).

Bean, broad, dwarf French, runner
Beetroot
Broccoli
Brussels sprouts
Cabbage, summer, autumn, winter, spring
Carrot
Cauliflower
Celery
Cucumber for greenhouse or frame growing
Kale
Leek
Lettuce you may like to grow a cabbage and a cos variety
Onion for pulling young for salad use
Onion maincrop, if you are not growing this crop from 'sets'
Parsnip
Pea you may wish to grow early and maincrop sorts

Radish most radishes are grown for summer use; there are also
  radishes for autumn/winter use
Spinach if you prefer Perpetual spinach this may be listed in the seed
  catalogue as Spinach beet
Swede
Tomato if you intend growing tomato plants outdoors, choose a
  variety recommended as suitable
Vegetable marrow
Herbs most seedsmen sell some herb seeds. Parsley is usually raised
  from seed
Onion sets, Shallots, Potatoes order them if you cannot buy them
  locally. Few mail order seedsmen offer potatoes. (500 gr/1 lb each
  of onion sets and shallots should be sufficient. Potato 'seed' is sold
  in minimum 3 kg (7 lb) lots. Make sure you do not over-buy seed
  potatoes

Appendix 4

Glossary of garden terms

All trades and hobbies have their own jargon. The newcomer to the growing of garden food crops learns the meaning of many garden terms as his or her own knowledge of the subject increases. Not only do other gardeners use special gardening jargon in conversation but the terms are used in gardening books and periodicals.

Annual weeds Weeds which grow and mature in one year

Aphis, aphids Plant lice: greenfly, blackfly

Blanch, blanching, blanched In vegetable growing the terms mean to make white. Maincrop celery is invariably blanched. In home-freezing the term refers to the short boiling period followed by quick cooling

Blight Usually refers to a fungal disease of potatoes and tomatoes

Bolt Premature flowering, 'running to seed'

Brassicas The cabbage plant family

Canes Can refer to bamboo sticks popularly used as plant supports or to the stems of some fruits . . . blackberries, loganberries, raspberries, currants

Catch crop A crop grown on land which is temporarily vacant. Lettuces and radishes may be grown and harvested in a bed reserved for the season's winter greens or tomatoes

Cloches Glass or plastic movable miniature 'frames'

Club Root A common and serious fungal disease of brassica roots

Compost This has two meanings. The word usually refers to *garden compost*, the cheap manure the gardener makes from mixed waste materials. The term sometimes refers to special home-made or bought propagating and growing mixtures such as Levington Composts

Crown The part of a plant which is at soil level or just below it. Generally a perennial plant. Loosely used to mean a complete rootstock for replanting, e.g. rhubarb

Cultivar A term used by some writers to describe what are spoken of
as 'varieties' in this work and by most amateur gardeners, e.g.
'Arran Pilot' (potato), 'Moneymaker' (tomato), 'Royal Sovereign'
(strawberry) are cultivar names

Dibber A pointed (usually wooden) tool for planting

Drawn Plants which have inadequate light or which are crowded
tend to become tall and spindly

Drill, seed drill A shallow furrow usually made with a hoe

Earthing Up Drawing up or placing soil around vegetables. Main
crop celery is always earthed up; many gardeners *earth-up* potato
plants

F1 Hybrid A plant obtained by controlled fertilization of seed.
F1 hybrids are bred for special attributes, e.g. heavy cropping or
resistance to disease

Fertilizers Chemical or non-chemical plant foods. Often an
unnecessary expense. If chemical fertilizers are used improperly the
garden soil may become sick

Forcing Hastening plants by growing them with protection and often
with artificial heat. For chicons, chicory is usually *forced*

Frost pocket A low-lying area where frost may often ruin the blossom
of fruits

Gall A lump on a root or stem as made by Turnip Gall Weevil

Garden frame A box-shaped container with a removable glass or
plastic top. Most garden frames are unheated and are referred to as
cold frames

Graft Various fruit varieties are grafted on (united to) special
rootstocks

Green manures Plants grown on vacant land for digging into the soil
before they are mature and woody

Half-hardy Plants which cannot withstand very low temperatures.
Seeds are not sown in the open garden until warmer conditions
prevail; alternatively seedlings are raised with protection and the
young plants are hardened off before being set out in the open
garden

Harden off Acclimatize tender plants to lower temperatures and
harsher weather conditions

Haulm Top growth of some vegetables particularly beans, peas and
potatoes

Head Developed top growth of such vegetables as cabbage,
cauliflower, celery, lettuce

Heavy soils Soils which have a high clay content

Heel-in To plant temporarily in the ground. Not final planting

Herbicides Chemical weed killers. Their use is not recommended in the kitchen garden or on an allotment site

Intercropping A space-saving kitchen garden practice. All vegetables need adequate space for good growth but occasionally two different vegetables may be grown closely together. Examples are lettuces or summer cabbages grown between rows of dwarf peas or plants of trailing vegetable marrows guided around blocks of sweet corn

Laterals Side growths of plants

Legumes Peas and beans

Life of seeds Vegetable seeds are expensive and although seeds of some vegetables retain their vitality for several years it is the established custom among gardeners to invest in freshly-bought seeds each season. Unless packed in special containers and housed at special temperatures seeds gradually lose vitality. Parsnip seed should always be new, fresh seed

Lights Windows of a greenhouse and the top, movable part of a garden frame

Light soils Soils which have a high proportion of sand or gravel

Lime Can be oxide, hydroxide or carbonate of lime prepared from either chalk or limestone. Lime is used by gardeners to prevent or correct soil acidity. Over-liming is a common, wrong gardening practice

Liquid feeds Plant foods in water solution. They may be home-made or bought for dilution

Maidens A fruit tree in the first year after grafting and before initial pruning has been undertaken

Matted bed A way of growing strawberries. Remontant strawberries are always grown by this method

Mulch A cover placed around plants or in which plants are set out. Garden compost, farmyard manure, straw and peat are good mulching materials

Nursery bed Where brassica seedlings are replanted and left to grow larger before being planted in their permanent growing positions

Pelleted seeds The seeds of several different vegetables are now offered as pellets. The coating is often clay

Perennial weeds Weeds with a life of three or more years

Pesticides Pest-killing dusts and sprays. The gardener is advised not to use any which are potentially dangerous to himself, his family or his pets. Pesticides which may harm wild life generally should also be avoided

Pinch-out Stop growth of a shoot, using the fingers. In tomato growing small shoots on standard-type plants are entirely removed. The tops of plants of climbing beans are shortened by 2·5 cm (1″) or so

Planting out The planting of seedlings in their permanent growing positions. The seedlings of less hardy vegetables are *hardened-off* if they have been raised with protection

Pollinator In vegetable growing this means bees and other insects which by transferring pollen from flower to flower effect pollination. In fruit growing it may also mean this but may refer to varieties of apples, pears and plums from which pollinating insects collect and transfer pollen

Remontants A French word used by gardeners for late summer/ autumn fruiting strawberries

Restricted forms Some tree and bush fruits may be grown in restricted forms – cordons, espaliers and fans

Rootstock That part of a fruit tree on to which the variety to be grown is grafted by nurserymen

Rotation of crops Not all vegetables need as much plant food as others. Potatoes, Brussels sprouts, cauliflower and winter cabbages are greedy feeders. Results are best where these are grown in ground which has recently been dressed with large quantities of well rotted farmyard manure or garden compost. There will be adequate plant foods available in the residues of the manure or compost for less greedy feeders like lettuce, broad, French and runner beans and many other vegetables. Cabbages and their kin (the brassicas) and potatoes should be rotated around the garden or allotment so that brassicas do not follow brassicas nor potatoes follow potatoes. Rotating one's crops is also believed to be a way of preventing a build-up of dangerous root diseases such as Club Root of brassicas. It is not easy in the small garden to follow the sort of rotation advised for larger gardens and allotments. This is as follows:

First year	Second year	Third year
Potatoes	Brassicas	Other vegetables

In the following season potatoes are grown in the patch of ground where the Brassicas were grown in the previous season; the ground is enriched (and limed where necessary) for Brassicas to be planted where other vegetables were grown. All other vegetables are produced where potatoes were grown in the previous season. So the rotation proceeds season after season.

Runner plant The small plants which form on runners and take root around established strawberry plants

Saving seeds Results from seeds saved from most vegetables are unlikely to be good. Exceptions are dwarf and runner beans and tomatoes. Do not try saving seeds of any F1 Hybrid vegetables. Do not packet home-saved seeds until they are absolutely dry. Store the seeds in a cool, dry place

Seed bed A specially prepared site for seed sowing. The bed may be in the open garden or under cover. In kitchen gardening brassicas, leeks and lettuces are often raised in a seed bed and the seedlings are transplanted

Seed leaf First leaf or first pair of leaves; often different from the *true leaf*

Set, set-out To plant

Sets Sometimes means seed potatoes but more usually means immature onion bulbs bought for planting in the garden

Soil mark A change in colour at the base of fruit trees and bushes. The mark indicates the depth at which the tree or bush was growing before it was dug up for sale by the nurseryman

Standard In vegetable growing the term is usually restricted to tomato plants which are grown as tall plants as opposed to dwarf bush plants. The fruit grower recognizes large, tall trees as *standards*; gooseberry bushes are obtainable as grafted standards

Stopping Removing the growing tip by pinching-out

Suckers, sucker plants Plant growths arising from buds on the roots of shrubs and trees

Successional cropping This means keeping the garden or allotment under cultivation throughout the season. As soon as one crop has been harvested the ground is made ready for the immediate sowing or planting of another, different crop.

Successional crops Crops which are sown little and often throughout the growing season. Examples are lettuce, radish, spinach

Thin, thinning A reduction of the number of seedlings in containers or in the soil. Some fruits (e.g. apples, gooseberries) may also be thinned

Tip To prune by 2·5 cm (1″) or more using the fingers, a pruning knife or secateurs

Trace elements Chemicals vital to plant growth but needed in very small quantities. Most garden soils contain sufficient quantities of trace elements

Transplant Dig up and replant elsewhere. Many seedlings may be transplanted

True leaf Typical leaf of a plant; often different from the *seed leaves*

Truss A cluster of flowers or fruit; more usually restricted to flower and fruit clusters on tomato plants

Tuber A swollen underground stem; potatoes are typical tubers

Viruses Various diseases in the sap of plants; usually transmitted by aphids

Index